D0837083

HARDLY
WORKING
AT RELATIONSHIPS

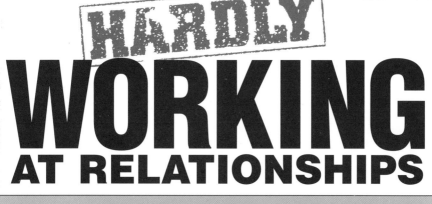

The Overachieving Underperformer's Guide to Living Like You're Single When You're Not

Written by Chris Bishop
Illustrated by Mike Pisiak

SIMON SPOTLIGHT ENTERTAINMENT
New York   London   Toronto   Sydney

SIMON SPOTLIGHT ENTERTAINMENT
An imprint of Simon & Schuster
1230 Avenue of the Americas, New York, New York 10020

An EYE book

Text and illustrations copyright © 2005 by EYE Quarto, Inc.
All rights reserved, including the right of reproduction in whole or in part in any form.
SIMON SPOTLIGHT ENTERTAINMENT and related logo are trademarks of Simon & Schuster, Inc.

Conceived, designed, and produced by
EYE
276 Fifth Avenue
Suite 205
New York, NY 10001

Editorial and Art Direction: Michael Driscoll
Cover and Interior Design: Sheila Hart Design, Inc.
Copyeditor: Katherine Devendorf
Proofreader: Adam Sommers
Production: Chris Morran

Publisher: William Kiester

Manufactured in China
First Edition   10   9   8   7   6   5   4   3   2   1

Library of Congress Cataloging-in-Publication Data
Bishop, Chris, 1972-
Hardly working at relationships : the overachieving underperformer's guide to living like you're single when you're not /
by Chris Bishop ; illustrated by Mike Pisiak.
    p. cm.
"An EYE book."
ISBN 1-4169-0023-3 (alk. paper)
1. Dating—Humor. 2. Man-woman relationships—Humor. 3. Mate selection—Humor. I. Title.
PN6231.D3B57 2005
818'.602—dc22
2004027293

Acknowledgments
and Dedication

I know no one reads these things, but maybe as a society we should all agree to start. Oh, do what you want. First, a huge thank-you to Michael Driscoll, my good friend and point man at EYE. You inspire me. Stop it. Also at EYE, Will Kiester. I can really tell by your notes that some woman hurt you deeply. Buck up, soldier. Thanks are due also to my publishers, to Mike Pisiak for his hilarious illustrations, and to Sheila Hart for her terrific design. To my buddies Jonathan Berry and Levi Douglass, who, when I quizzed them about women, had absolutely nothing to add. To Fred Hough, thank you for your endless stories about your wife. Don't let her read this. Thanks to the lovely Katy Monti, who hit me every time I told her the title of a chapter. And of course, thanks to all the women on the planet. Except you, Jenny Fitzhugh of 1263 Willowbrook Road, Green Bay, Wisconsin. You know why.

This is for my mother—the only woman I never lied to … much.

Contents

Section V: The Workplace

Section VI: Diet and Exercise

Section VII: A Night Out with the Guys

Section VIII: Holidays and Observances

Section IX: Her Parents

Section X: Fighting

Section XI: The Vacation

Section XII: Love

Section XIII: Marriage

Section XIV: The End of the Affair

Introduction

This guide is for novelty purposes only. It is not meant as a handbook for any real-world relationships. A strong and healthy love life can only be achieved through a nurturing and selfless devotion to your partner. The author and the publishers strongly encourage you to seek out genuine— Okay, your girlfriend has probably stopped reading this. We all know the real reason you bought this: Your lady's been driving you crazy and you want a few tips to help ease the pain. Well, nice purchase, amigo. This guide will assist you in traversing the rocky landscape that is dating. So read on. And if your woman does find this book and confronts you with it, tell her that it was a gag gift from Doug in the office. That Doug. Turn it off once in a while.

There are three basic types of boyfriends. The *Overachiever* is the doting, henpecked man who does whatever his girlfriend says, always picks up the check, and forever lives in fear of upsetting her. The Overachiever is perpetually unhappy, though he convinces himself he's not.

The *Underperformer* is barely aware that he's in a relationship. He does nothing to please his girlfriend and is always one "You're blocking the TV" away from getting dumped. Ignore the smirk; he knows he's on the brink, and his happy act is a hollow one.

The *Overachieving Underperformer* has a canny knack for the careful balance that a functioning relationship requires. This knowledge enables him to do the absolute minimum in order to keep his girlfriend happy, his wallet full, and his time free. It's the perfect situation—everybody wins. Especially him.

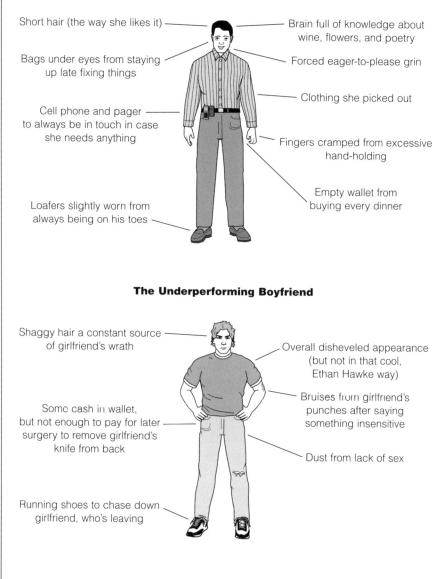

The Overachieving Boyfriend

Short hair (the way she likes it)

Brain full of knowledge about wine, flowers, and poetry

Bags under eyes from staying up late fixing things

Forced eager-to-please grin

Clothing she picked out

Cell phone and pager to always be in touch in case she needs anything

Fingers cramped from excessive hand-holding

Empty wallet from buying every dinner

Loafers slightly worn from always being on his toes

The Underperforming Boyfriend

Shaggy hair a constant source of girlfriend's wrath

Overall disheveled appearance (but not in that cool, Ethan Hawke way)

Some cash in wallet, but not enough to pay for later surgery to remove girlfriend's knife from back

Bruises from girlfriend's punches after saying something insensitive

Dust from lack of sex

Running shoes to chase down girlfriend, who's leaving

The Overachieving Underperforming Boyfriend

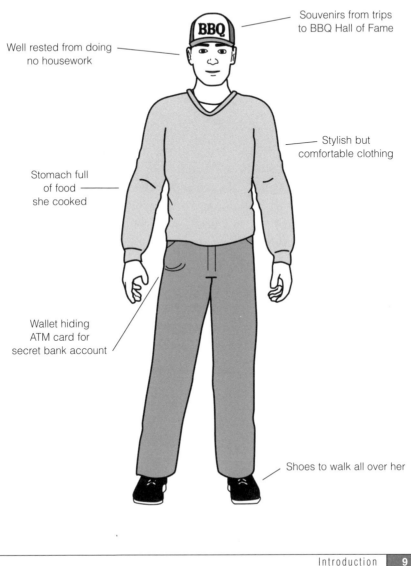

Souvenirs from trips
to BBQ Hall of Fame

Well rested from doing
no housework

Stylish but
comfortable clothing

Stomach full
of food
she cooked

Wallet hiding
ATM card for
secret bank account

Shoes to walk all over her

Section I
Finding the Right Gal

Finding a woman is easy. Finding the right woman is hard. Your ultimate happiness depends on your selection. The Overachieving Underperformer thinks of it like buying a car. He pores over her specs until he can make an informed decision. Does the exterior have cracks? Does she have a lot of miles on her? How big are her headlights? How much junk will fit in the trunk? Can you park her in the garage until you need her again? You can't just kick the tires and see if there's enough gas to get to Vegas. Unless, of course, you expect to leave her on the side of the road and never look back. . . .

Those of you who already have a girlfriend don't need any help finding a woman. But for you fellas who are looking, or want to trade in your old model, the next few chapters should get you pointed in the right direction.

Chapter 1

Beauty Fades . . . Slowly

People claim that beauty fades, which, of course, is true. That cruel beast Time marches on, and no one is immune. No plastic surgery, liposuction, or baby tee from Urban Outfitters can stop its effects. What people don't tell you is that beauty fades slowly. If you're planning to stay with a woman for the long haul, you must understand that the best-looking old women were once the best-looking young women. Rarely do unattractive women bloom in their golden years. There's a reason the ugly duckling story is a fairy tale. It just doesn't happen.

Now, if the woman's current looks are adequate but you see her starting to fade (her ass is growing like the national deficit), you can date for a few months while she's still within the acceptable range. But keep a close eye on her and be prepared to end things as soon as her appearance really starts going south. Who knows—maybe she'll surprise you and never ugly up.

Of course, the best thing you can do is find someone really attractive.

Obviously, this is easier said than done. So, to be more specific, you need to find the most attractive woman you can get. Don't settle for a woman who has a face with "character." She's one acne scar away from living under a bridge and frightening children. And thanks to fashion magazines and the unrealistic expectations they set for women to live up to, there are a million beautiful women out there with low self-esteem available to you.

Check out what she looks like without makeup. If the war paint covers up the fact that she could stand in a cornfield and scare off blackbirds, dump her.

Chapter 2
Some Friend-ly Advice

One factor to consider when choosing a girlfriend is what your buddies think. While your friends are a bunch of immature morons, they are still a good litmus test for whether a girl is a "keeper." So you need to ask yourself: Do your buddies wish your girlfriend were dead? The answer can save you hours of heartache down the road.

If your cronies can't stand your special lady, they won't want to hang around. And since your woman can sense when your pals are giving off the death vibes, she in turn will hate your friends. This animosity creates unneeded friction for you.

Recognizing the Signs That Your Buddies Hate Your Girl:

- They groan every time you mention her name.

- When invited to a free meal, they ask if she's going to be there.

- They suddenly have to go home early when you meet them at a bar with your lady.

- You miss a lot of parties that they "forget" to tell you about.

- They scream like giddy teenage girls when you tell them you're flying solo tonight.

- They try to set you up on dates with other chicks (even their sisters).

- They burn her effigy.

So make sure your friends are cool with your lady. They know the truth. You're too close to see it, or blinded by sex. Trust them or say good-bye to them.

Overachieving at Underperforming

The lucky few, the crafty ones, are able to score the dual prize of a girl who is both attractive and tolerated by his friends. These rare females offer benefits for all the males involved. If you're the boyfriend of a woman who's built, quiet, and agreeable, your benefits are obvious; if your friends can stand her, they're liable to benefit too, because hot women tend to surround themselves with other hot women.

Hot women tend to hang around with other hot women. Your friends know this.

Chapter 3
A Glimpse of the Future

A long-term relationship can be a great thing. But how do you know if she'll age well? The best way to find out is to test-drive her mom.

You see, your potential girlfriend will turn into her mother in twenty-five years. Genetics don't lie. If her mother is a sweet, older, but still attractive version of her, you've just struck relationship gold. Keep her. But if her mother has packed on more pounds than a British bank, toss her back.

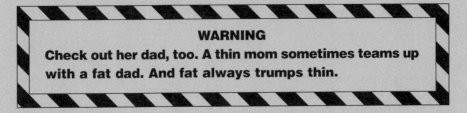

WARNING
Check out her dad, too. A thin mom sometimes teams up
with a fat dad. And fat always trumps thin.

Also, monitor her eating habits. Does she just adore fried foods? Can she go one day without a king-size Snickers? Does she butter her Skittles? Her parents may be thin, but her sweet tooth could translate into booty-not-so-licious.

Judging Her Family Portrait

Good   **Bad**

She may not inherit her mom's ass, but you should be forewarned that there are other traits her mom can hand down. Here is a list of other things to look for in her mother:

① Check Out Her Hair
Is it thin and limp? Is it prematurely gray? Does she wear a wig? Women can go bald too. And you don't want to be stuck with a female Uncle Fester.

② Check Out Her Skin
Is it clear? Are there age spots or is it excessively wrinkly? Cracked, wrinkly skin could be due to sun damage or lack of care, habits that may have been passed down. Keep after your girlfriend about her skin care.

③ Check Out Her Eyes

Does she wear contacts, glasses, or even bifocals? Can she drive at night? Do you really want to have to spend a fortune on eye repair? Or to squander your golden years helping your old lady learn Braille?

④ Check Out Her Teeth

Are they healthy and white? Are they false? Loss of teeth is usually from lack of care. Does your girlfriend have the same lazy tendencies?

⑤ Check Out Her Posture

Does she stand up straight? Is there a hunch? Bowed or hooked posture is decidedly unattractive.

If grandma's still in the picture, check her out too. Granny's swollen ankles and wrinkled smile might be her only legacy.

Chapter 4

Smart but Not Smarter

Intelligent women can be wonderful. You can discuss politics, religion, philosophy, and even sports with them. They usually have a career of their own. And most importantly, they use reason rather than emotion to guide them. (Unless you're dealing with body image. Even Marie Curie cried while standing on a scale.)

But unlike being too rich and too thin, there is such a thing as too smart. The Overachieving Underperformer (OU) code tells us that the perfect woman has an IQ about one point below yours.

You want to be the manipulator, not the manipulat-ee. A sharp girl can't be prodded into doing the things you want to do. In fact, clever girls will make you their pawn. Without knowing it, you will be attending ballets, symphonies, and poetry readings. And somehow it will be your idea.

A brainy gal can see through your bullshit. Any lie, exaggeration, or false emotion will be exposed, and you will be made to play the fool.

Adequate

Good

Very Bad

Chick Tricks

Spendthrift or Miser:
What Kind of Woman Can You Afford?

If money were no object, most women would have an airplane hangar housing only their shoes, and only the size of the hangar would vary. When choosing a potential mate, you have to ask yourself: What kind of woman can you afford? For example, a bus driver can't afford to date women who will order the eighteen-dollar peach martini. And investment bankers don't have to date women who "borrow" Sweet 'N Low packets from Sizzler.

Let's face it. Your income determines the type of woman you'll date. Here's a quick chart to help you out:

Tax Bracket	Woman You Can Afford
Unemployed to Car Wash Attendant	⟶ None to Crack Whore
Mechanic to Realtor	⟶ Motel Maid to Waitress
Lawyer to Plastic Surgeon	⟶ Secretary to Working Actress
Movie Star to Internet Billionaire	⟶ Hotel Heiress to Any Human, Alive or Dead

Chapter 5

She's Got . . . Personality:
How Much Hotness Are You Willing to Trade?

Okay, so you want to date an international supermodel. Whoa, not so fast. A woman who looks great on the outside doesn't necessarily look great on the inside. For the most part, the hotter the woman, the more difficult she is to deal with. You have to decide how much you're willing to put up with, and how much hotness you're willing to trade for a gal with an agreeable personality. Every guy is different: Some have the stamina and fortitude to put up with the capricious, self-absorbed pageant winner, others would just as soon date a hobgoblin if it meant not having to put up with any crap. So take a minute to consider how much you can tolerate from an attractive woman.

Here is a series of scenarios to aid you in making your decision.

At a sporting event, your ideal girlfriend will:
  a sit through the game with you, quietly encouraging your team.

  b barely tolerate it, constantly question what's going on, and demand to leave at halftime.

  c paint her face with the team colors and insist on cooking the burgers and dogs at the tailgate party.

At a bar, she will:
  a drink a little but stay sober enough to drive you home.

  b get falling-down drunk on your dime, yell at you for wearing that stupid shirt, and leave to go to a club with her friends.

  c buy you and your boys shots, make out with you in the bathroom, and take you to get late-night pancakes afterward.

When you're at work, she will:

a call you once during the day to see how you're doing and let you know what time dinner is planned.

b call you constantly to ask you inane questions, complain about people at her work, and chide you for not taking her out to that new Italian place with the singing waiters.

c wait for you to call to see if you need singles for the strip club.

When the two of you are choosing a movie, she will:

a make a decision based on fairness and mutual enjoyment.

b demand to see the subtitled period piece, or nothing.

c buy a big tub of popcorn because she knows how hungry you get while watching explosions and car chases.

In the bathroom, she:

a takes her time to look good and seldom holds you up.

b wastes hours and couldn't care less if the dinner reservation was ten minutes ago.

c washes and primps quickly and makes sure the car is fully gassed and pointing toward the steakhouse.

If you answered "a" most of the time, you're best off dating a woman with moderate good looks.

If you answered "b" most of the time, you'd better be dating a very attractive woman.

If you answered "c" most of the time, you're probably kissing Sasquatch—but who cares!

Section II
The Date: General Principles

There are numerous pitfalls to avoid while on a date; it's rarely as simple as just "dinner and a movie." But an Overachieving Underperformer can easily negotiate this relationship mine field.

Chapter 6
First Things First: Early Dating Strategies

We all know the scene where a guy walks a girl to her door and gets a kiss on the front porch before he sheepishly runs back to his car. That's fine for 1952, when your grandfather came a courtin'. But you want a little more than a quick peck on the cheek.

1 Find Out if She's Religious

If you want to know if she's prudish, ask her if she's pious. It doesn't necessarily mean she's not going to worship your tongue later that night, but loose women don't tend to frequent churches, synagogues, and temples as much. If your date is carrying a Bible or quoting Allah, chances are, you'll be sleeping alone.

2 Talk About Sex

The topic of sex creates an atmosphere of sex. If she's thinking about it, you're halfway there. Just don't go overboard. There is a fine line between a seductive conversation and a creepy one.

3 Loosen Up with Alcohol

Grab a few drinks while on your date. It reduces inhibition and can help you with those first-kiss jitters. But don't go too far. You don't want to get too drunk, and you certainly don't want her to get too drunk. It leads to sleepiness and ending a night early. Also, have at least two bars in mind to visit during the date. Even if she's a light drinker, she'll have one drink per venue. And if you get her to bar number two, it means the date is going well. But if she wants to hit bar number four, she's probably an alcoholic nightmare.

4 Rent a Horror Movie

You'll both be sitting in the dark on the couch. It's the perfect place to start smooching. And a horror movie gives her reason to jump into your arms. The heightened atmosphere creates giddy tension. She will be snuggling with you in no time. As a bonus, horror pictures are usually outlandish goofs. She won't care if she's missing the predictable ending because she's making out with you.

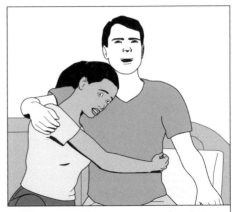

Horror movies are second only to motorcycle rides in their ability to make girls cling to you.

5 Show Her You're a Man

Women are hardwired to pick their potential mates based on prowess. So all you have to do is show her how good you are at something. If you can crush a baseball, take her to the batting cages. If you can rebuild a V-8 engine, take her into your garage and show her your muscle car. If you can underwrite the hell out of corporate tax law, then . . . buy a Porsche.

6 Go for the Kiss

Sometimes you just gotta take the shot. Move in for the kiss. She already agreed to go on a date with you, so she must like you on some level. Never go home kicking yourself for not trying. If you're afraid to dive in to the tonsil hockey, start with a little preliminary hand-holding. The contact should loosen her up a bit. If she pulls away, you can probably forget the kiss. But if she lets it linger, it means she digs you. You should be swapping spit in no time.

Chapter 7

The Un-Occasioned Gift:
A Sucker's Bet

Many young Romeos think it's nice to buy a little something for their dates—typically flowers or a box of chocolates. Or worse, both. Although this may seem generous and romantic, it's actually detrimental.

1. Chocolate is a little old-fashioned, and nowadays a little odd. On the one hand, it does say, "I don't think you're fat. Eat up." But unfortunately it also can say, "I don't care enough about you to mind if you gain twenty pounds." If there's a good way and a bad way your woman can read meaning into something, you can count on her reading the bad meaning. No chocolate.

2. Flowers are only for apologies and funerals. So when you show up with a bouquet for "no reason" or "just because," she won't believe you. She'll think you did something wrong and felt so guilty about it that you had to make up for it with peonies. No flowers.

3. A single rose may seem like a thoughtful gesture, but deep down your girl is really thinking, "He's cheap and he doesn't care about me enough to drop an extra twenty for the full dozen." No single roses, jackass.

4 Also, gift-giving sets a precedent. On the next occasion another little present may be expected. And ultimately she'll be disappointed if it's not there, subconsciously asking herself, "Why no flowers this time? Does he not like me anymore? Maybe he's cheating on me. I'll bet it's that slut Veronica at the gym. I'm going to kill them both. Where did I put my razor-sharp machete and/or gun?"

Think before you give.

What She's Thinking...

| **"Does he want me to get fat?!"** | **"What did he do wrong?"** | **"Cheap bastard!"** |

Give her nothing. She won't have a reaction if there's nothing to react to. And how easy is it to do nothing?

Chapter 8

Dining Out:
The Dutch Know How to Treat a Lady

"Gourmet" to you means your burger isn't served on a plastic tray. Your girlfriend, however, probably thinks a fancy restaurant with "jackets required" is the way to dine. Sometimes you have to bite the bullet and take her out.

"I made a reservation for 7:00."

1 Choose or Lose

If you are absolutely forced to eat out, you should at least select the restaurant. The best way to go where you want is simply to choose ahead of time. Merely explain to her that you made a reservation and that's where you're going. Women actually prefer when men have planned things out. They don't like to ask you, "Where do you want to go for dinner?" And they hate it when you say, "I don't know, where do you want to go?" Indecision is weakness. Having dinner reservations is good. Having dinner reservations at a cheap joint is better.

2 Not on My Dime

Establish beforehand that you'll handle dessert and a movie and your girlfriend will pay for dinner—a tradeoff that appears equitable on the surface. At dinner, get an appetizer or two, then order a main dish that comes in heaping portions. Share as much of your entrée with her as possible. (This should not be hard to accomplish; women generally love eating off other people's plates because they think that food doesn't "count" on their daily calorie tallies.) While you're stuffing yourself and forcing food on her, tell as many rambling stories as you can, stretching the meal out to at least two hours, preferably three. If you're successful, (a) you'll have gotten a huge, tasty meal on her dime; (b) she'll be too stuffed for dessert; and (c) it will be too late to catch a movie.

WARNING

The I-forgot-my-wallet approach is not a viable option for use with a girlfriend. This should be reserved for special, one-off instances, like blind dates where you wish you were actually blind.

③ Pay You, Pay Me

If you can't convince her to pay, try the every-other method, where you each take turns paying for the meal. That way when it's your turn to pay, you can take her to a cheaper place. If she suggests Maison D'Expensive, you explain that you had French for lunch. If she pitches Muy Pricey Mexican, you had tacos the night before. All you have to do is wait until she proposes a reasonably priced place and then agree. Even praise her choice: "I love that ribs joint. Good thinking, honey."

Choose the restaurant based not only on price, but also on proximity to your bedroom. If the date goes well, you want to be ready for anything.

Take turns paying for meals.
Make sure it's her turn when you go someplace nice.

The Thursday-Night Drinks Date:
Cutting to the Chase

The Thursday-night drinks date is one of the greatest inventions since the push-up bra. It involves no paying for dinner. It involves little commitment. It involves alcohol. You meet, you drink, you go home and go to bed. After all, you have to work in the morning. As often as possible, try to get your woman to agree to this kind of date. It's cheap, it's casual, and you don't have to worry about getting steak sauce on your good T-shirt.

The Thursday-night drinks date saves you:

  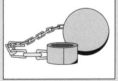

Time   **Money**   **Commitment**

Chapter 9

Home Cooking:
Making Lazy and Cheap Seem Quaint and Romantic

Most of your home-cooked meals are probably prepared with a micro-wave, but you should be able to cook at least one thing well. Whether it's fajitas, spaghetti marinara, or fried chicken, master something and whip it up for her. It's cheaper than a restaurant, but it seems quaint and romantic. Plus, you've already got her back to your place. It's win-win. Of course, there are some rules you should follow before stepping into the kitchen:

1 Cook Something You'll Both Enjoy

If she's a vegetarian, do not whip up your famous beef stew simmered in chicken broth with just a dash of endangered bald eagle. She might not be as excited about it as you are.

**Presentation is everything:
Spend a few dollars on placemats and
cloth napkins. These things turn a simple
supper into fine dining, and can be used
again and again.**

2 Make Plenty

There's nothing worse than an empty pan when she's asking for more. Also, make at least two vegetables in case she hates one. Fries count.

❸ Set the Table

Candles, cloth napkins, and glassware without a beer logo. These things turn a simple supper into fine dining.

❹ Play Some Music

Something light and airy like soft jazz. Nothing takes her out of the mood faster than dueling banjos or gangsta rap, so stick with the Miles Davis.

❺ Buy a Bottle of Wine

You may not be able to tell pinot grigio from strawberry schnapps, but you should have a little table wine. A safe bet is anything over ten bucks. If you're still confused, the clerk at your local wine store will usually be more than happy to make a recommendation tailored to whatever you're preparing. An added bonus of buying a bottle: It gets you both nice and tipsy.

❻ Make Dessert

It can be as easy as opening a pint of ice cream. But don't be boring. Don't just hand her a Twinkie. Crumble your own Oreos into a dish of toffee ice cream. Drizzle chocolate and caramel over strawberries and pound cake. Make it your own. And hey, you can save that whipped cream for later.

❼ Screw Up

If you mess up a part of the meal like the main course, she'll remember it endearingly as something you really tried to do for her but couldn't. After all, you're just a man. This mistake sets her up as the cook of the house, and you will rarely, if ever, have to set foot in the kitchen again.

WARNING

Make sure your dog is tied up or out back. If TV has taught us anything, it's that an anxious mutt can ruin any formal occasion. "Oh, Tiger."

If you've done everything right, you'll both be happily full and she'll be giving you that dreamy look that says, "I want to make many, many children with you."

If you want to avoid actually cooking for her, get take-out and pretend you were the chef. It'll probably taste better, too. Arrange the food on one of your own plates and throw out any evidence, like bags, containers, and the receipt. Dirtying up some pots and pans will help sell this one.

Chapter 10

Movie Night:
You Pick the Flick

Unfortunately not every feature film has explosions, car chases, and panty raids, and it's these exceptions your girlfriend wants to see. She wants love, romance, and story lines. Luckily the Overachieving Underperformer can escape from the doldrums of Jane Austen Presents . . .

1 Rentals

A great way to avoid seeing anything with Glenn Close in it is to rent two movies when you're at Video Mart. Let her pick any movie she wants. It can be a plotless art picture, a funereal tearjerker, or even the dreaded foreign film. Don't worry about it. Pick out the movie you'd really rather see. Just make sure there is an obligatory love scene in it. (Lesbian scenes count.) When you get the videos home, ask if you can watch your movie first. You just want to get it out of the way, then you can see the true cinematic masterpiece. After your movie is over, she will be too tired to sit through another flick. If she does want to watch it, you be the tired one. Either way, you're free. Make sure you return both movies the next morning. "Honey, the late fees are where they really get you!"

2 Cinema

Going to see an action flick on the big screen can be great. Going to see Hugh Grant cry his way through 1930s France—not so good. Sadly for you, her kind of movies don't tend to sell out, so you can't use that as an excuse. But there's a handful of strategies you can use to avoid her films.

Planning your excuse for not seeing her choice ahead of time will help avoid any unnecessary movie-selection controversy.

ⓐ "Ow, my back." Art house theaters are usually rundown places. Complain that you need a nicely cushioned seat. You refuse to sit on a lump of foam rubber for an hour and a half.

ⓑ Blame the critics. Tell her you read an article that panned the film. Use words like "dreadful," "poorly directed," and "thumbs down." Then hope it doesn't win an Academy Award and prove you, er, that critic, wrong.

ⓒ Mess up the time. If you know the movie starts at seven, show up at seven thirty. Be shocked and angry. Oh well, as long as we're here, let's go see Supermodel Car Wash at seven forty-five.

ⓓ Seen it. Lie and say you've seen it. This can be difficult. The movie must already have been out for at least a day, and you have to be able to give an opinion about it. Something vague, like "I thought it fell apart in the third act. I mean, they really hit you over the head with the symbolism. But I liked it." Newspaper or Internet reviews can help you here.

ⓔ Nap time. Go see it with her when you're extremely exhausted. It's dark, there are no screaming kids, and classical music will probably play throughout. You should be able to sleep. Your lady may be angry when it's over, but hey, you wanted to do something with her and you tried, so how can she really complain? And her bitterness over your sleepiness is invariably less than her anger would be if you dragged her to the movie you wanted to see.

Chapter 11

Celebrating Feminism:
How Women's Lib Saved Mankind

Susan B. Anthony is not just a face on a crappy coin. She was a famous feminist who vied for equality and helped women get the vote. Nice going, Sue. But with all this liberation comes a trade-off. You can exploit this.

1 Dutch Treat

Make it known early on in your relationship that you truly believe in women's equality. That's why you won't be paying for her lobster dinner. If she doesn't chip in, she'll be stomping on the graves of those who fought for her right to own property. If she wants equality, she can pay for it.

2 Etiquette

Good-bye to opening doors for your lady. Tell her that you know she is capable of doing it herself and that you think it would be unjust to think otherwise. Tell her to not think you're rude, you're only doing it out of respect for her gender.

3 Heavy Lifting

If she really believes in equal rights, she won't make you do any kind of labor that she finds too dirty or too intense. No longer are you available to help her move, change her oil, or reach that dish. "No, the blue one."

Section III
The Date:
Contingency Planning

The Boy Scout motto is "Be prepared." And what these kerchief-wearing young men know is that every good plan has a backup plan, or at least a method of bailing out when things go south. The Overachieving Underperformer is prepared for any unforeseen problems that may occur while out on the town with his girl.

Chapter 12

Going Nowhere:
Making Your Exit

Sometimes a night out with your lady can quickly go into the toilet. Your car won't start, the movie's sold out, or the Greek deli you were going to take her to was closed down by the Health Department. A woman doesn't want to deal with unexpected problems. It isn't attractive, and it certainly isn't going to get you upstairs for a "nightcap." So if you sense the date is souring, don't waste time trying to resuscitate it, just bail. There are easy ways you can do this.

① Get Sick

A fake illness can let you escape with a little grace. You can try headache, nausea, or fever. These can be easily faked and can't be questioned. As an added bonus, she might even put you in bed and try to nurse you back to health. But if you're a little riskier—or if you want to disgust her to the point of never seeing her again—tell her you have severe diarrhea. It isn't sexy, but you might gain points for being honest. Nowadays women aren't squeamish debutantes prone to fainting. Some may even find it refreshing that you can open up to them. So don't be shy about a little dysentery.

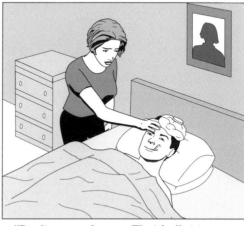

"Don't worry, honey. That ballet troupe will be back next year. What's important is you getting better."

② Emergency Call

Nowadays most cell phones can be set to vibrate, so you can easily pretend to get a call without hearing a ring. The best emergency is a non-medical one. You don't want to tell her your mom got hit by a car and you gotta run; she'll just want to tag along. Make it a work emergency. It's your boss calling, and the big client didn't get the latest update on the [last name of favorite quarterback] account. You have to go. She'll understand and appreciate your importance at the office.

③ Run

Don't look back.

Chapter 13

Your Place vs. Hers:
Pros and Cons

It's a sad truth that sleeping with a woman often requires one actually sleep with her. That being a given, the following OU principles should be considered before you pose the question, "My place or yours?"

❶ The Pros of Your Place

- It's your comfort zone. You don't have to feel like a guest worrying about using coasters or keeping her bichon from humping your leg or barking during sex.

- You set the mood. You control the music, the lighting, and the drinks. If you feel like Duran Duran under Christmas lights with mimosas, then go for it.

- If she's never been there, you can give her the tour. The tour is just a way to get her into your bedroom. And you really want her in your bedroom. It's where you keep your bed.

When you get her in your room, sit on your bed and tell her you want to show her a photo album or other prop. Hold it between you, examine it closely, turn and kiss. You'll be rolling around on your bed in no time.

❷ The Pros of Her Place

- It usually smells good and she has soft linens.
- If you're having a drink, it's on her dime.

- Your mess, not your cleanup. If you trash the place in a drunken orgy, you get to go home without wiping the strawberry jelly off the ceiling.

③ The Cons of Your Place

- You must clean it. Let's face it: You don't like picking up your dirty socks, let alone making your bed and scrubbing your toilet.

- You don't want her knowing where you live until you've confirmed that she is not a Psycho Chick. A Psycho Chick is one who never leaves you alone. For example, leaving angry letters written in her blood on your front door is a good sign you're dealing with someone who should be institutionalized rather than in your dating pool. The best way to avoid her knowing your address is not to take her there.

- There is no escaping. If things are going poorly, you can't leave.

④ The Cons of Her Place

- Her TV is a mere nineteen inches, and she doesn't have Dolby surround sound. How are you supposed to watch a movie with this caveman technology?

- The food sucks. Everything is diet, light, low-carb, or fat-free. Where are the frozen corndogs?

- What the hell is that sock filled with lavender in her top dresser drawer? While this shouldn't necessarily interfere with your getting your game on, its mere presence is an unwanted distraction and a constant reminder of the crude comforts of your slovenly home.

Chapter 14

Home Alone:
Outfoxing the Sleepover Trap

Let's say you've successfully made the transition to bed buddy. Depending on your obligations the next morning (early tee time, morning tailgate party, or just sleeping in), you must now decide whether you're going to spend the entire night with her or Houdini your way out of there.

① How to Get Out of Her Place

The strategies discussed in Chapter 12 can often be applied here as well. Another, more delicate, option is to screw with her sleep. Cough, sneeze, kick, snore—these are all irritating habits; no one wants to sleep next to a noisy, fidgety blob. Keeping her up all night tossing and turning will ensure you'll never be invited back—but there's the rub: Is never being asked into her bed again really what you want? Probably not.

Getting out of her place is as simple as making her want you to leave.

The solution is to employ these irritating tactics selectively. For those nights when you really can't bear to be in her presence for another thirty seconds, or can't stop fantasizing about your perfectly worn-in pillows and universal remote control, turn on the leg kicks and loud sighs. When she asks what's wrong (if you're annoying enough, she won't be able to bear more than fifteen minutes of this), tell her you've just got a lot on your mind tonight—it's that pending visit by the district manager at work, or your little sister's news about another out of wedlock child. Be creative, and play to her particular sympathies. When managed correctly, this tactic can not only get you a free pass out of bed, but can also explain why you "just need some time" to yourself that weekend (i.e., it's Playmate Night at the strip club on Saturday, and the Super Bowl is Sunday afternoon).

➋ How to Get Her Out of Your Place

If you don't want to wake up to her puffy face and skunk breath, you must do something bold. And unless you're dating a brainless playmate, the early-morning meeting lie is far too transparent—and it doesn't really work when your job title is cashier at Arby's. So you need to try something new: creating an inhospitable sleeping environment.

Filth is your friend here. When you establish a setting that is more than uncomfortable—it's disgusting—she will volunteer to leave. And because, as the Chaos Theory teaches us, the universe tends towards disarray, this atmosphere is easy to maintain: just don't do anything.

Don't clean those dishes. Don't wash those sheets. Let trash pile up. Hide some food and let a weird smell develop. Tell her your toilet's broken and it won't be fixed until tomorrow. Turn up the heat or turn off the air conditioner. Tell her you can't sleep without your sleep-aid: a white-noise soundscape. Does she prefer "Static Hiss" or "Aphids Mating"? Burn incense with cloying, overbearing scents. Anything that will get her to get out.

If, however, you find that the atmosphere necessary to drive her out is so unpleasant that you can't stand it either, you should bear in mind that it isn't that bad waking up with a woman in your bed. There's morning sex, pancake breakfasts, and gaining her trust. So weigh the pros and cons before you commit to turning your place into a pit of repugnance. You have to live there, after all.

Section IV

Living Together

Sharing your living space with a lady is completely different from sharing your bed. The first thing you'll notice is that your space is compromised. You won't even believe how much stuff she has. You will be staring into your closet at five hundred pairs of shoes that look exactly the same. Also, she will quickly replace your stuff with more tasteful furniture. Your beer keg end table will be replaced by something rattan. Your armadillo alarm clock will be shelved for something "less crappy." You'll also have to clean. Everything. Who knew you had to mop under the fridge? And no more leaving the dishes piled up for a week. Clothes must be folded and put away. You also can't just eat dinner—you have to ask her if she's eaten or planning to eat, and then schedule your meal according to her whim. You may be splitting the rent, but life just got a lot harder.

Luckily the Overachieving Underperformer knows many tricks to help ease the pain of cohabitation.

Chapter 15

Housework:
Your Sworn Enemy

With the possible exception of obsessive-compulsives, everyone hates housework. There's a reason it's called "chores." Dusting, mopping, and doing the dishes isn't fun. It's work. Fortunately there are ways to be lazy and not be blamed for it.

Convince her that slovenliness is simply your nature.

1 Allergies

You can attribute almost anything to allergies. Rub your eyes and explain that you couldn't possibly mow the lawn with your hayfever. The pollen count is up, so you can forget about dusting. Make sure you have props lying around such as antihistamines or even a surgical mask.

2 Sports Injury

Use your tennis elbow to preclude you from ever having to wash, scrape, or rub down anything. You will be on the couch "healing" if she needs you.

3 Hiding

This is by far the coward's way out, but it works. Find someplace in the house where she won't find you and hide out. The garage is a good choice. You just have to ask yourself, how long are you willing to inhale gasoline fumes to avoid making the bed?

4 Let It Rot

If you do no cleaning, she will. This always works. If you let every chore pile up, it will become so unbearable that she'll eventually do it. Let the dishes stack up to the sky. Overstuff the trash can. Live like the Irish. Most women are neat freaks and will break long before you will. Eventually she'll come to realize that you're just a messy guy, and she'll have to live with it. Welcome to the promised land.

Chapter 16

Controlling the Remote:
Television Turf Wars

In the 1950s there were three channels, and men and women still couldn't agree on which show to watch. Nowadays, with television's diverse programming and thousands of choices, it is nearly impossible to see eye to eye. You can either buy another TV, or you can compromise. Sitting through one of her whiny made-for-TV movies about single moms trying to cope could buy you five hours of Sunday football. You just have to remind her, "Hey, I sat through your show about feelings, you can sit through me screaming at the TV about how the defensive line's got a hole in it the size of a Buick. C'mon, number 78, put a hand on him!"

This works, but it does mean letting her watch some of her shows. If you'd rather that she never has control, you must annoy her to the point that she'll relinquish her TV rights. During her show, you should:

❶ Run Your Mouth

Talk during the show, and she will want to kill you. When she asks you to quiet down, tell her that she always complains that you never communicate enough. She can't have it both ways.

❷ Eat

There's nothing more annoying than someone crunching on chips during your favorite show. Find the loudest snack you can and go to town.

❸ Ask Pointless Questions

Who's the guy in the mustache? Is this set in Santa Barbara? Where do I know that actress from?

➍ Adjust the TV Settings

Constantly change the color, tint, brightness, sharpness, and volume. Tell her you're just trying to make it better. She'll wish for your swift death.

➎ Toss a Ball

It's insanely distracting when someone throws a ball up in the air near your head. Keep it up.

➏ Fidget

Constantly change positions on the couch. Claim you can't find a good spot and ask her to switch several times. Never settle down. It will drive her insane, and she'll eventually learn that she can't watch her programs around you.

**Just because you've agreed to sit through one
of her programs doesn't mean you have to actually watch it.**

Overachieving at Underperforming

Every man wants to fart freely without his lady looking at him like he punched Jesus. Breaking the fart barrier is a delicate process, and the key is to start small and build. You begin with a light burp. Immediately apologize and label it as being rude and unlike you. She should casually dismiss it. After a few days bring out a larger belch. Once again apologize, and blame the soda or beer. A few days later you'll be belching the alphabet in front of her. She might think it's gross, but play it off as youthful fun. That's when we move into the darker territory—the fart zone.

The first time you fart in front of her, make sure you're alone so she doesn't play up the fact that you're revolting. Without an audience she has no one to complain to. A tiny fart, sometimes known as a "squeaker," is your best choice. It was a mistake; you're only human, after all.

Some time later, complain of a stomachache and let a longer one out. Act embarrassed and blame Mexican food.

Next, try out a tester—a fart that you definitely pushed out. If she freaks out, take it slow. If she laughs, let out another. Continue until you feel comfortable letting them loose like gunfire. Pretty soon you'll be waking her up with bed shakers that make the plants wilt.

Chick Tricks

Naps:
They're Not Just for Toddlers

Dreamy Sunday afternoons on the couch watching golf . . . It makes you sleepy just thinking about it. A quiet nap is the perfect way to kill an hour after having a few beers or a heavy lunch. But when a woman is in your home, you will have no time to slumber. You cannot "waste" your day away. There are activities to be undertaken, craft fairs to see, wilderness trails to hike, art openings to attend. There's not a moment to spare. So if you want your siesta, you must be one thing: grouchy. Every time you miss a nap, act cranky and irritable, like a two-year-old. Whine, throw things, snap at her. When she complains, feign remorse and explain to her that without an hour's rest every weekend, you feel the same way she feels when she hasn't eaten in a while. She'll know exactly what you mean. From then on, she will insist you get your precious nap, maybe even fluff up the pillows for you.

Chapter 17

All That Glitters . . . :
The War of Cleanliness

The War of Cleanliness rages all over the house. One of the major fronts in this struggle takes place in the bathroom. For you, the bathroom is there to move bowels, empty bladders, and occasionally shower. For her, it's also a repository for thousands of essential products and tools to make her look presentable. She has hair curlers and straighteners, makeup applicators and removers, moisturizing lotions and grease-removing pads. She spends more time in that little room than in any other part of the house, so she expects it to be in tip-top shape. You, on the other hand, couldn't care less that there are microbes living in the bath mat or that the toilet is permanently stained yellow.

But you must remember, her day starts in the bathroom. If she's unhappy in the morning, it carries on throughout the rest of the day. So why not take a few steps to keep her happy?

① Superficial Sparkle

Take a sponge and wipe down the toilet. Do a good enough job that all visible areas are clean. You don't have to eat off it. Just wet the sponge, give it a wipe, and you're done. Billions of tiny life forms may be breeding on the underside of the toilet seat, but she'll never know it. Instead, she'll see that superficial sparkle and think, "Aw . . . he cleaned. I think I'll bake him some brownies."

When it comes to housekeeping, it's only necessary to clean what's visible.

② Never Let the Paper Run Out

Make sure there's plenty of Charmin for her to squeeze. Nothing ticks off a woman more than reaching for the roll and finding nothing there. So stock up. And when you use the last sheet, replace the roll. In the bathroom, as in life, thirty seconds of effort now is roughly equal to thirty minutes of laziness later.

③ Don't Move Her Stuff

It looks like a jumble of crap to you, but there's probably a method to her makeup madness. If you move her hair dryer from the top of the toilet to under the sink, let her know. Or else you'll get an angry call at work wondering why you threw out her BlastDry 2000.

④ Use Time Wisely

If you have any business to do or doo, make sure it's not done at the same time as her morning ritual. She has every second in there planned out and doesn't need you poking around looking for that sandwich you left in there last night.

Section V
The Workplace

Some people work to live, others live to work. But the one thing the industrious businessman has in common with the guy napping in the stockroom is a pesky girlfriend. She prevents them from having a quiet, annoyance-free work environment. The Overachieving Underperformer can avoid this.

Chapter 18

Hold My Calls:
Keeping Her Out of Your Work Life

Whether you work in a law office, at a construction site, or on a flying trapeze, your woman will inevitably manage to telephone you. Her calls drive you and everyone you work with crazy. How many times can she call to "just check in"? It interrupts your work and bothers your coworkers. So how do you stop these calls?

① Set Parameters

Tell her to call you between noon and twelve thirty, or after five. If she misses that window, tough. She can tell you all about the skirt she got on sale when you get home. You're busy earning the money to pay for it.

Embrace the digital age. Tell her to e-mail rather than phone. A pile of e-mails can be handled quickly at your convenience, and you never have to engage in her annoying small talk.

② Your Boss Will Fire You

Explain to her that your boss is a hard-ass and doesn't like your mixing personal stuff with business. She won't want you to be fired—who will buy her drinks? Or houses?

WARNING

If you avoid her too much, she will physically come to your office for a "visit." This presents many dangers: For starters, she may find out what you really do, not just what you told her, Mr. Assistant Manager. She also may attempt to strong-arm you into cleaning your workspace just like she does at your home. And finally, she can embarrass you in front of your coworkers. One overheard "sweetie-poo" and you just got yourself an office nickname.

---

③ Never Be In

Pretend to be constantly traveling or otherwise out of the office. If you're not at your desk, she cannot reach you. (Note: This will not work if your office is a Sno-Kone shack. She knows you're not at the Cleveland branch.)

Chapter 19
Hiding Your Money:
Playing Down Your Net Worth

Never tell your girlfriend how much money you make. The less she thinks you have, the less she'll expect you to spend. Convincing her that you don't have the dough is easy.

1 Downsize Yourself

If she likes you for who you are, it shouldn't matter. If you're the senior vice president of marketing, tell her that you're a junior manager of marketing. If you're an auto mechanic, tell her you're an assistant auto mechanic. If you're a chammy boy at the car wash, tell her the truth. If she finds out your real position—surprise, you got a raise! You didn't tell her because you were waiting for it to be official.

2 Show Her a Crappy Bank Balance

Find the most pathetic discarded bank statement at any ATM and leave it lying around for her to find. Once she sees you only have seventeen dollars, she won't be ordering the caviar salad the next time you're out.

3 Have a Secret Account

Slowly siphon money into a secret savings account. Have all the paperwork sent to your office and immediately destroy any evidence of its existence. Don't get sloppy or lazy about this. If there's a paper trail, she'll follow it to your clandestine fund.

If she finds your secret stash, tell her you were planning a surprise European vacation for the two of you. Suck it up and take her. Then start a new fund and be more careful this time.

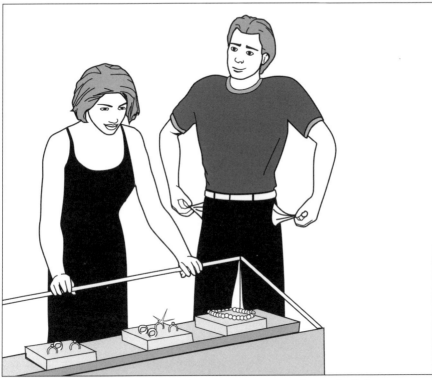

Play poor. She can't spend money you pretend you don't have.

Chapter 20

The Sugar Mama:
Mooching off Her Success

Men are by nature competitive. They compete over anything—the remote, highest scores on video games, or even how many olives they can stuff in their mouths. The idea of dating a powerful, more successful woman fights against their very being. They like being the breadwinners in the relationship.

This is idiotic. The Overachieving Underperformer knows that dating a successful woman can be like winning the lottery. Here's why:

1 She's Too Busy to Yell

A woman who is consumed by her career has little time to bitch at you for leaving the toilet seat up.

2 She Doesn't Want to Talk About Her Day

When she gets home, the last thing she wants to do is discuss work. She just wants to unwind with a bottle of wine and maybe a little TV.

3 She Doesn't Expect You to Pay for Everything

If she wants something, she'll buy it herself, and when the dinner bill comes she'll fight you for it, not ignore it and apply her lipstick. She'll also insist upon a higher level of restaurant, bar, etc. You, of course, will go along with her wishes—to make her happy. And because the drinks are free when you fly first class.

4 She'll Buy You Stuff

Clothes, golf clubs, even scuba diving trips to Mexico. She'll have no qualms about plunking down a couple of pesos so you both can have fun. "Ooh, a manta ray."

Section VI

Diet and Exercise

Today, most people are health conscious. They may not be physically fit, but they know a cheeseburger isn't going to lengthen their lives. Your girlfriend is no different. She wants to be thin and healthy too. Your job is to encourage her without being a jerk.

Chapter 21

"You Look Fat in That" and Other Subtle Asides

Sometimes your girlfriend needs a gentle nudge in the direction of dieting or exercise. Here's a quick list of things you should throw into your everyday conversation to keep her thinking thin. Can you pick which ones are acceptable and which ones are an instant trigger for tears?

- "I don't care what society says, your body shape is fine."
- "I don't think I could lift you if I tried."
- "You know, I'll bet I can fit into your jeans."
- "I remember when I used to be able to get my arms around you."
- "Wow, I've never seen a woman put away that much food."
- "How dark was the dressing room when you tried on that two-piece bathing suit?"
- "Are you pregnant?"
- "Honey, that shirt is too young and hip for you."
- "Please don't sit in my lap. Ow! I can't feel my feet!"
- "Look at her. You used to look like her."

Obviously you can't get away with using any of these remarks. Unless, of course, you're "joking." So don't forget to add "I'm kidding! I'm kidding!" Her first reaction may be anger, but the seed has been planted. She'll own a TummyBlaster by week's end.

Ogling a Woman in Front of Her

You hop out of your car and an angelic gift from God steps into your line of sight. Your eyes linger for a moment on that soft skin; those tan, shapely legs; the way her hair bounces. Then your girlfriend notices and you're smacked for leering. There must be a better way to check out the opposite sex without getting a sock to the gut and an earful from the old lady. Try these tricks:

1 Wear Sunglasses

Dark or mirrored lenses hide the eyes. But you must do more than just wear them; you must position your head so you can see the hot woman only out of the corner of your eye. Staring straight on is a dead giveaway.

2 Never Turn Your Head

If an attractive woman passes through your field of vision, do not swivel your neck to follow her. Instead, let her pass, then casually tie your shoe and turn your head in one fluid motion. Better yet, find a reflective surface in which to ogle her indirectly.

3 Pretend to Search the Crowd

Let your eyes drift from person to person as though you are scanning several people, and one just happens to be a busty redhead who can't possibly be wearing a bra. You're just people watching, not watching her graceful splendor. Oh my God, she's yawning!

And if you do get caught, you've still got an out. Just say something like, "Why do women want to look that skinny? It's gross and unnatural. I prefer a woman with curves." Follow that fib with a pat on her backside and a kiss on the cheek. Then put your sunglasses back on, jackass.

Chapter 22

Complimenting Her Looks:
The Value of the Outright Lie

Just as properly worded insults can send your girlfriend an important message about her shortcomings, kind words can be employed to your advantage too. For instance, the easiest way to get her out of a bad mood is to compliment her looks (even if she doesn't deserve it). She will eat it up. Here's a quick list of things to tell her to put her in a good mood.

- "Whoa, did you lose ten pounds?"

- "Who replaced my girlfriend with Catherine Zeta-Jones?"

- "Yum."

- "Did I just step on a time machine or did you get younger?"

- "Somebody call the fire department because you're smoking hot."

- "Oh my God, my heart just skipped a beat."

- "You should definitely wear that more often."

- "With that skin, you could be a model."

- "Hubba-hubba. Somebody took her beautiful pills."

- "I want you."

Bask in her happiness. Then use it to get something from her that you want.

Chapter 23

The New Food Pyramid:
Using Fad Diets to Your Advantage

Fad diets crop up every year. No red meat, no carbs, only eat foods that are green—she's tried them all. Rather than poking fun at her, you should encourage her eating obsessions.

Think about it. If she can only eat organic grains, you won't be going out to eat all the time. If you never go out to eat, you never have to pay for dinner. Do the math. Let's say you go out twice a week. You spend an average of thirty dollars each time. At the end of one year, you'll have spent $3,120! That's enough to buy a billiards table, a pinball machine, and an extra copy of this book.

On the flip side, you too can benefit from being on a diet. Except your diet is a lie, and when she's not around, you can eat what you want. Tell her that you only consume specific low fat foods, and you can't take her out to eat because prepared foods don't have

Encourage her fad diet and you'll never have to buy her a big meal again.

the right carb to fat ratio. Make up the rules to fit the situation. She can't complain because it's a health issue. One the contrary, she will probably encourage your new healthy eating habits. She might even join you on the "diet," which means she loses weight while you gain money. It's having your cake, but she's not eating it too.

Chapter 24
Golf and Bowling:
The Lazy Man's Cardio and Weight Training

Your woman may encourage you to stay fit as well. Her nagging you to lose the love handles can be a hassle, but there are easy alternatives to hitting the gym and running five miles every morning. The OU idea is to find "sports" that require minimal effort and provide maximal excuse.

① Darts

This old pub game blends hand-eye coordination and balance. It works mostly the triceps and biceps. Plus, you get to drink while doing it.

② Golf

This entails walking miles in the sunshine and hitting a tiny ball as far as you can. It works the legs, the arms, and the back. Plus, you get to drink while doing it.

③ Bowling

This sport involves lifting and slinging a sixteen-pound weight. It works all the major muscle groups. Plus, you get to drink while doing it.

④ Fishing

This involves sitting quietly for long periods of time with the occasional wrist flip. If you hook a big one, it can work arms, legs, and back. Plus, you get to drink while doing it.

Convince her all sports are exercise.

Find your favorite and keep at it. The best exercise routine is one you can stick with.

Section VII
A Night Out with the Guys

As Bob Marley said, "No woman, no cry." How many times has your girlfriend been a wet blanket when it comes to having a great time? Did she demand to go home from a toga party early? Or force you to rent a crappy movie and stay in on St. Patrick's Day? Or make you go garage sale hunting for that perfect end table during March Madness? How much wicker can one woman need?

Every so often you have to get away from her and take some "me" time. You need to chug cheap margaritas with your buddies and belt out a drunken version of "Brown Eyed Girl" without your girlfriend shaking her head in the corner.

You need a night out with the guys.

Chapter 25

The Escape

In order for a rocket to travel beyond the constraints of our atmosphere, it must reach a speed of seven miles per second or about twenty-five thousand miles per hour. It requires incredible amounts of focused energy and power, and several teams of scientific geniuses working in perfect harmony. Success is a statistical miracle. In order to escape from your girlfriend for one night, you will need better luck.

You must first convince her that you have a harmless, legitimate reason for leaving. In response to your request, she will ask you a series of seemingly simple questions. The questions, of course, are anything but simple. Each has a veiled meaning, so you'd better know what suspicions they are really hiding, and the right way to respond to them. The following pages demonstrate the proper way to handle these tricky Q&A sessions.

Correctly answering her questions will still only get her to grant you a conditional release. After giving her consent, she'll want to know the details. Where you're going exactly, what time you'll be returning, and who you'll be with—basically, a complete breakdown of your schedule to the minute. And once you're out, she'll expect real-time updates via cell phone, and reserve absolute veto power over any last-minute changes or unforeseen keg parties. But these obstacles are manageable too. The Overachieving Underperformer can handle any contingencies in order to have his guys night out.

What she asks:

Translation:

"Where?"

"Are you going to a bar? Is it even remotely close to a strip club? If I were to show up unannounced and surprise you, would you really be there?"

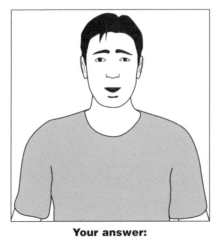

Your answer:

"No matter where we go, I'll be sad because I'm apart from you."

What she asks:

"When?"

Translation:

"When will you be home? Will you be playing 'Video Golf' until four in the morning? What time can I expect you to drunkenly grope me when you finally do show up?"

Your answer:

"I don't know. It always seems like an eternity when I'm away from you."

What she asks:

"Who?"

Translation:

"Are you going to be with your buddy Steve the Drunken Idiot who I hate? Will you be hanging out with other women? You'd better not be out with that skank Judy from your office who has a crush on you!"

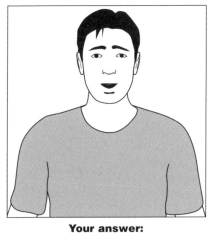

Your answer:
"I wish it was just me and you."

What she asks: **Translation:**

"Why?"

"Why don't you want to stay here with me?
Am I not good enough for you? Why
would you need to spend time in a bar
ogling the waitress if you're taken?"

Your answer:

"Our time apart makes every second we're together mean more to me."

Chapter 26

Legitimate Reasons for Being Unreachable

Technology has given us many great advances: Surround sound, slow-motion instant replay, and Internet porn. Unfortunately it has also given us a society where people aren't unreachable. Cell phones keep us in touch no matter where we are. And she doesn't care if your cell phone batteries ran out, if you were in a service "dead zone," or if you left your phone at the office. She wants to be able to get ahold of you, or, more importantly, keep tabs on you. Plus, if you didn't have your phone, why didn't you find another way to contact her? There are pay phones, home phones, walkie-talkies, CB radios, semaphore flags, carrier pigeons, and skywriting. You must never be incommunicado.

Luckily the Overachieving Underperformer has a few excuses at the ready for avoiding this constant contact.

❶ Gone Fishing

Explain to your lady that you will be doing a little night fishing. It's an important serene escape for you that helps clear your head. For you, it isn't about the mastery of man over beast. It's a spiritual journey. With beer. You will return around two in the morning after the fish have "gone to bed." Also, any good angler knows that noise scares the fish, so unfortunately you will be on all-quiet mode. That means no music, no talking, and no phone calls. And you're a catch-and-release guy, so you won't be returning with any fish.

If you tell your girlfriend you practice catch-and-release, she won't expect you to come home with a fourteen-inch trout when you return from "fishing."

② Boring Work Party

Sometimes you have to go to work-related parties. These are invariably painful events where you have to be on your best behavior— no one wants to go to them. Your girlfriend is no exception. Tell her you're going to let her off the hook and go it alone. You'll just hobnob with the boss for an hour and leave. Ask her please not to call, because you don't want to seem anxious to leave, and a phone call may seem rude. When you return home late, tell her that the boss pulled you aside and forced you to do shots with him. How could you say no?

Tell her you're going to a boring work party.
She'll invariably take a pass.

> **WARNING**
> Don't forget to wash any bar stamps off your hands.
> They are a dead giveaway that you weren't at that
> Saturday night funeral like you said you were.

③ Concert/Movies

You obviously can't talk on a cell phone during a rock show or motion picture. This gives you a two- to three-hour window. Enjoy it.

④ Turn the Tables

Constantly call her. Tell her every tiny detail of what you're up to, including what kind of drink you're having, the comfort level of the bar stool, and the color of the bartenders' T-shirts. After an hour and a half, she will be so sick of your calls that she will ask you not to bother her anymore unless something interesting happens. The key here is to make sure it sounds like you're having a boring time: "Joe dropped a peanut on the floor and that turned into this whole discussion of our favorite kind of peanut butter. Then I started to say I liked strawberry jelly instead of grape, and that turned into a whole jelly vs. jam thing. . . ." Just ramble on until she stops you. The phone won't ring again all night.

Keep a can of potpourri or odor remover in your car. It can get rid of the smell of cigarettes, alcohol, and stripper perfume.

Chapter 27

Swearing to Tell the Truth
. . . to a Point

The Italian philosopher Marcus Fabius Quintilianus once said, "A liar needs a good memory." What he meant was, in order to not get caught, a liar needs to recall everything he said—every nuance, every detail—or he could falter, get tripped up, and betray his deception.

Great sound bite, Quint, but we all know how hard it is to keep track of trivial details once we get an elaborate and entertaining alternate reality going. The truth is, elaborate lies, deceit, and collusion are often unnecessary. When telling your lady about your night out with your buddies, in most situations you are better off sticking to the "truth" or something that vaguely resembles it. Here are four tips to keep you from slipping.

❶ Shut Up

Your girlfriend can poke holes in your story more easily if there's more story to work with. So say as little as possible. If you don't say anything, how can you be accused of lying? If she smells champagne on you and asks what it is, say, "Champagne." Nothing more. Don't mention you bought it for the six sorority girls with the short skirts. (This may seem like common sense, but you would be surprised how many guys get in the doghouse because they thought the truth would "set them free.") And if she presses you for the details, stick to succinct answers and don a slightly confused look, like her line of questioning puzzles you: "Why do you smell like champagne?" "I just told you. Because I drank some." "Why did you drink some?" "Because it was available." "Why did you order it?" "To drink it." "What were you celebrating?" "I just wanted to drink it." This deconstruction will drive her crazy and she will eventually drop it.

Other short answers to questions:

a *"Where did you go tonight?"*
"Out."

b *"Who were you with?"*
"The guys."

c *"Why were you out so late?"*
"Because of the time."

d *"Were there other women there?"*
"I didn't notice."

e *"Where's your shirt?"*
"Gone."

She won't be happy with the brevity, but she'll eventually get frustrated and stop with the interrogation.

2 Stick to the Truth or Something That Vaguely Resembles It

Sometimes you need to omit details of a night out in order to spare your girlfriend's feelings, or to spare her from giving you a sound beating. When recalling the night's events, there are certain things you must leave out if you don't want her wagging her finger at you in the morning. Remember the five Ws.

a **Women.** If you talked to a woman, no matter how innocently, leave it out. She hates when women talk to you, and she really hates when women talk to you and she isn't there.

b **Wine.** Okay, you drank seventy-five shots of Jäger. Congratulations, Mr. Churchill, you're a drunk. Just don't tell her about it. Unless your girlfriend is a nineteen-year-old college sophomore with an Adam's apple, she's not going to be impressed.

c Whuppings. No need to fill her in on the bar fight you lost. Skip it. Where'd you get the bloody lip? Stupid car door.

d Wagers. Lost your wallet at a cockfight? Bet a mint that you would run naked through the cemetery at midnight? The only sure bet is that she'll be upset, so zip it.

e Weddings. Witnessed a buddy's drunken marriage? Accidentally got hitched to a Russian émigré trying to get her green card? Say "I do" to not saying a thing.

3 Embrace the Fabrication

Even the boldest among us at times find ourselves in situations where denial, avoidance, and omission won't work. In situations like these, you have to lie. You have to look your girlfriend straight in the face and tell her the biggest whopper of your life.

The key here is embracing the fabrication: Internalize the lie. If you convince yourself that you really, truly were tying balloon animals at the orphanage instead of doing a pub crawl with your fraternity brothers, then you can lie convincingly. Imagine the false scenario. Think about how you would react to the situation. Construct a mental picture of yourself going through the events of the lie. This allows you to believe the story, to sense where the odd detail may be useful, and to convincingly retell your tale as if it had actually happened.

4 Learn to Recognize a Lie and Avoid Those Telltale Signals

Once you've learned to recognize a lie in others, you can avoid their mistakes. Many women can pick up on men's "tells," so if you can hide your subtle giveaways, women are more inclined to believe you. What are the common signs of a liar?

a No eye contact. Liars tend to avoid looking you right in the eye. So make good eye contact when fibbing.

b Touching your chin/rubbing your brow. Liars make nervous movements such as playing with their hair and crossing their arms. So keep still.

c Excessive denials. Liars say "no" over and over again and repeatedly deny allegations. They tend to go overboard with their vehement insistence that they did not and would not do such a thing. This is to be avoided. Be firm but not fervent.

d Inconsistencies. Some liars revise their stories through the course of the telling, and change minor details accidentally. You should not be one of these people. Stick to your original story.

e Building Barriers. Liars often position themselves so that a desk or a chair is in front of them. This is a subconscious way of hiding from the untruth. So stand near your girlfriend and deliver the lie at close range.

f Smugness. Liars act self-satisfied and feign an air of pretension. So check your thesaurus and do whatever the opposite of smug is.

Plan your evening out opposite her girls night out. When she's out carousing with her friends, you will be free to go out carousing with yours. Except instead of having a glass of wine, you'll be drinking beer. Instead of going to a club and dancing, you'll be drinking beer. And instead of getting a late-night bite, you'll be drinking beer.

Chick Tricks

To Lie or Not to Lie:
An Instructional Chart

The best advice is: Don't lie if you don't have to. Are you really going to get in trouble just for hanging out with your friends? If the answer to that one is yes, your girlfriend had better be a supermodel. Otherwise, it's generally only when you cross the line with jail time or alcohol-induced nudity that you need to whip out the big fib. The chart below sets forth some basic guidelines for when, and when not, to lie.

Offense	What to Do
Drank too much	Tell the truth.
Drank too much and punched a nun	Lie.
Drank too much and punched a nun in self-defense	You're already lying, so continue.
Kissed a Dallas Cowboys Cheerleader	Lie.
Kissed a woman who was a Dallas Cowboys Cheerleader in 1977	Shudder, then lie.
Kissed a Dallas Cowboys Cheerleader in 1977 and won't shut up about it	Get a new story.
Woke up outside	Tell the truth.
Woke up outside your ex-girlfriend's apartment	Lie.
Woke up outside your ex-girlfriend's apartment handcuffed to a tree naked	Seek help for alcoholism, then lie.

Chapter 28
Sneaking Back In

For some reason, live-in girlfriends get angry when you arrive home at four in the morning on a Tuesday. They want to know where you were and what you possibly could have been doing out so late. And unless you're a professional raver, you really don't have a leg to stand on. The only way to avoid this conversation is to sneak back in.

Tiptoeing back into bed without being noticed is a difficult task, especially when you've knocked back a few. Many a man has tried and failed. Some have been betrayed by a squeaky floorboard, a confused and tired dog, or a dropped belt clanking to the floor. Others have misjudged their stealth capabilities or confused her silent, seething anger for sleep. Sometimes nothing can be done about a woman with insomnia and the desire to bust you. She will wait up until you arrive or until she receives proof of your death.

But there are ways to minimize your chances of getting caught creeping in after a night of alcohol and entertainment. Or, if need be, to minimize the damage done.

1 Be Quick
One of the biggest mistakes you can make is trying to slowly, painfully slink back into your house or apartment. Every second you delay is a chance for your girlfriend to hear you. Instead, you should quickly enter, make as little noise as possible, and hustle into bed.

2 Remove Your Clothes on Your Doorstep
Undress on your porch or outside the front door. That way you can climb

right into bed without additional noise time. Of course, you may want to make sure she isn't waiting for you on the couch, or you'll look like a crazy person. (This technique is also contingent on weather and neighborhood.)

③ Be Warm

Before you slide into bed with her, remember that she probably will jump out of her skin if your frozen toes touch her. So try and be nice and toasty when you get under the sheets. Use a portable heater or some hot water to warm up your extremities. You want nothing to disturb her dreams about fat-free ice cream.

④ Change the Bedroom Clock

When you crawl into bed, pretend to be setting the alarm, but merely change the time to a more reasonable hour. When she asks you what time it is, tell her to see for herself. If she's groggy from sleep, she will be confused enough to believe it. Once she nods off again, change it back to the correct time.

⑤ Phony Phone Call

Once inside your home and bed ready, take out your cell phone and call your home line. After it rings a few times, answer it loudly. Your girl should wake up. Enter the bedroom and tell her it was a wrong number. When she tells you that she didn't know you were home, you tell her you didn't want to disturb her, and you were just catching up on some reading. Once again, her confusion will assist you.

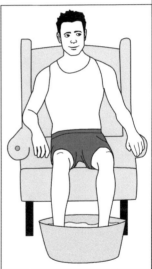

Frozen toes are a dead giveaway that you just snuck into bed. Warm your feet first.

Section VIII
Holidays and Observances

In a perfect world, the old adage "It's better to give than to receive" would be true. Unfortunately we don't live in that world. Everyone has their hands out, and your girlfriend is no different. When it's a special day, she wants a special something. And it can't be just any old crap.

Now, for specific occasions like birthdays, Valentine's Day, and those blink-and-you'll-miss-'em anniversaries, the Overachieving Underperformer faces a great challenge. He must figure out how to give her the best gift for the least amount and with the least effort—without leaving the couch, if possible.

Chapter 29

It's My Party, Really:
The Surprise Party You Didn't Plan

Most women don't like to celebrate the milestone of getting older— unless, of course, it means getting more attention. And what could be better than a surprise party? It's a significant gesture that says, "I'm willing to bust my ass to see you happy. Look how much I care." In reality, you can "plan" a surprise party with almost zero effort. It's as easy as picking up the phone.

Make sure you have a date picked out, and plan according to your convenience. The party will be enough to keep her happy; the scheduling should be such as to require the least amount of energy, money, and effort on your part. You may not like your girlfriend's friends, but the Overachieving Underperformer identifies their potential and takes advantage of it.

❶ The Setup

Go down the list of her friends until you find that busybody who always complains unless she gets her way—the one who is always controlling the situation: what movie to go to, what restaurant is the best, which bar to absolutely not step foot in. Every word from her mouth irritates you until you have myriad fantasies about her grisly death. Let's call her Helen. Explain to Helen that you want to throw your beautiful girlfriend a glorious surprise birthday party. Helen will take over faster than you can say, "I wouldn't mind a little help."

➋ Maintenance

Once you've got Helen's wheels turning, your job is simple: You must maintain contact with this woman. It must be perceived that you are throwing the party, not Helen. Ask her to keep the party simple—she won't. Let her know you only have a budget for beer—she'll rent a margarita machine. Explain to her that you don't really want decorations—she'll spring for Mylar balloons and color-coordinated party hats. Tell her you're baking a cake yourself—she'll remind you that she knows the guy who did J.Lo's wedding cake. Tell Helen you think you can fit everyone into your cramped apartment—she'll insist her back patio is perfect. Just keep dropping remarks about how you are throwing the party and you appreciate her assistance. Remind her that you're to be consulted on every decision. When Helen runs something by you, just nod your head and say, "What a great idea. She'll love it." The party will take care of itself.

Send out the invitations yourself with only your name as host, but tell guests to RSVP to Helen's phone number or e-mail address. This gives you none of the work with all of the credit. If you think Helen will get upset, send her a fake invitation that credits her as cohost.

➌ The Left Hook

Once the party is on track, you must do something that seems ridiculously counterintuitive: You must ruin the surprise! It's crazy, but it's absolutely necessary. The whole idea is to get complete credit for throwing the party, and the only way to ensure that is to control all the variables. Helen can't beat you to the punch if she's not even in the ring.

Here's how you do it: Sometime during the week before your girlfriend's party, when she inevitably asks what's happening for her birthday, tell her that you just want to stay home and watch the game.

When she protests, and she will, that's when you go ballistic. "I'm throwing you a surprise party, all right! Are you happy? Now it's ruined! After all the work I've done!" And don't be afraid to play off whatever was the last thing you got in trouble for. "That's where I was last Saturday—I wasn't getting drunk with my friends till midnight. I was planning your party!" She will get teary-eyed and apologize for ever having doubted you.

Then you must get your girlfriend to agree to act surprised for all those people you invited. When the actual party occurs, she'll be gushing to all her friends that she had no idea, and they'll be none the wiser.

④ The Follow-Through

To solidify your position as the perfect boyfriend, play host as the party commences. Take people's coats, bring out the cake, and thank everyone for coming. Do as much as you can early on so everyone can see, and ditch your girlfriend just before things die down so you can avoid cleanup.

Make sure you thank Helen in front of several guests for her help in putting this thing together. Just make sure your girlfriend is out of earshot, for instance when she's in the bathroom. This makes you seem like a gracious person while still maintaining full credit in your girlfriend's eyes.

⑤ The Payoff

When it's finally time to go, make sure you pull your girlfriend close and ask her if she liked her party. When she thanks you, nod and smile a smile that says, It wasn't easy, but you're worth it. You'll be able to raft down her tears of joy. Thanks, Helen.

Chapter 30

The Holidays:
The Twelve Days of Cheapness

Ahh, the holiday season. Twinkling lights, snow-covered hills, and eggnog flowing like the mighty Nile. For some the holidays are a joyous celebration with family, friends, and loved ones. But for most people they're a huge pain in the ass. December has the highest suicide rate of any month of the year. Is it holiday depression? Or girlfriends pushing their fellas over the brink? Gentlemen, it doesn't have to be so bad. Here are a few tips that will help ease the holiday blues without cutting into your green.

1 Decide on a Budget: The One-Day's Salary Rule

The diamond people have that brilliant two-month-salary scam for engagement rings. But what do you spend on her Christmas gift? Here's a simple formula. Take your weekly income, then divide it by five. That means if you make five hundred dollars a week, you should spend a hundred dollars on her. It's easy and you only have to work one day to get the money back. Now, if you don't have a job or you make less than two hundred a week, well, I'm sorry, but you must spend a minimum of forty bucks on her. Get a better job. And if you make more than five thousand dollars a week, please buy ten more copies of this book and use them as coasters for your diamond-studded goblets, Your Majesty.

2 Spread Out the Money

Make the value of the gift look like more than it is by buying several small presents. If your budget is one hundred dollars, then buy her one thing worth forty dollars and six things worth ten. Seven wrapped presents make you look seven times more generous than you are.

③ Find Out What She Wants and Change It

Women are very helpful. They will tell you exactly what they want and where to get it. The only problem is, diamond earrings from Harry Winston may not fall within the parameters of your budget. There is a solution. A good way to nudge her closer to your target price is to complain. Complain that the holidays always suck up hard-earned savings that could be spent on a tropical vacation with her. Complain that the spirit of the season is compromised by overconsumption. Complain that your holiday bonus isn't what you thought it was going to be. Complain early and complain often. Let on that if you could afford the moon, you would give it to her. You've now successfully lowered her expectations. Now you can give her the gift she always didn't know she wanted: the cheap one.

WARNING

If your girlfriend seems genuinely hurt or disappointed by your cheapness, abort your plan immediately. Bad gift anger lasts well into the new year. Have an emergency pricey gift ready to go.

Find a gift that both of you can enjoy, like wine or movie tickets.

④ WRAP IT!

A well-wrapped gift makes what's inside seem more valuable. Even if you have to spend a little extra time yourself, good wrapping turns a cheap gift into something special. But you might not have to do a

Wrap it wrong the first time.

thing if you employ a little ingenuity. Find the girl in your office who's knee deep in wrapping paper every year. Tell her you really want to make your girlfriend's gift perfect, and ask to borrow some paper. After she tells you how sweet you are and agrees, proceed to do the worst wrapping job ever. Don't cut enough paper, fold it wrong, put tape everywhere, and act frustrated throughout. She will invariably offer to wrap the gift for you. If she doesn't, then ask her to teach you how to wrap a gift. She'll wrap it, and all you'll have to do is nod your head every ten seconds. It's that simple. You also get the added bonus that your coworker will think you're sweet and will want to help you in the future.

⑤ Buy a Card

This seems easy but it's not. The card is the appetizer before the gift. It's the first thing your girlfriend opens, and it sets the mood. So when you pick it out, you have to take your time. No cartoons, no jokes, and no funny animal pictures. Find the simplest, most elegant card you can. And make sure it's blank inside. This is the key, because you will be writing a personal holiday note. And that's the easy part: Just find another card and copy its holiday message. Bingo, you're a sentimental genius.

⑥ Don't Clean Up

Congratulations, you survived the holidays intact. Now, usually there's a big mess to be cleaned up, but fear not, you won't be the tinsel janitor. Preplan a day of sports and movies with your friends, and insist that it's a tradition that was started way before she was in the picture. Your girlfriend won't be able to say no, and her new tradition will be picking up your mess. Happy Holidays!

All girls love jewelry, and all guys hate buying it. So take a creative approach—scour a few pawnshops looking for "antique" jewelry. These are just used items that you've "refurbished" (read: cleaned). It's a much better option than buying some ridiculously overpriced brand-new bauble, and the savings are passed on to you.

And if, for some reason, you've decided to marry your girl (see Section XIII), this is a great way to get the ring without the sting. When shopping for your girlfriend's engagement ring, you don't have to sell a kidney to make her happy. There are numerous jilted men and bitter women who are willing to part with these preowned beauties, so selection is wide.

Selecting a present for your girlfriend can be intimidating; improper selection has led to the demise of countless relationships. But, in fact, the principles of girlfriend gift giving are quite simple, with just three basic criteria that must be addressed in selecting an acceptable gift:

**The gift must be thoughtful
(not bought five minutes
earlier at a bowling alley gift shop).**

**The gift must be appropriate
(not a bottle of whiskey on her
five-year anniversary of being sober).**

**The gift must at least seem valuable
(not pulled out of a brown paper sack).**

Keeping these criteria in mind will help you with your selection
of gifts in the situations discussed in the following chapters.

Chapter 31

Massacring Valentine's Day

The real history of Saint Valentine is hotly debated by scholars. But since you didn't buy this book for some yawn-inducing historical dispute, let's just say the guy died and now you have to buy pink teddy bears every year. Let's also accept as truth that February 14 is far too soon after the holidays to be dropping a large chunk of change on your lady.

Of course, this is no challenge for the Overachieving Underperformer. There are three basic methods of handling Valentine's Day, none of which will massacre your wallet.

① The Evil Corporate Holiday

Is your girlfriend the liberal, tree-hugging, occasionally smelly type? Then this method is for you—just tell her that you don't celebrate Valentine's Day. It's a phony corporate holiday created by the greeting-card fat cats to make money off hapless rubes. Nowadays the corporate world can't be trusted, and you, for one, are not going to be exploited for some CEO's profit. This one could backfire if she senses how full of it you are, so it's vital that you really sell it to her.

a Be passionate. "Preying on consumers like we're idiot automatons! I won't stand for it!" The stronger your convictions, the more she'll believe your stand. But don't go overboard. No arched eyebrows or fist pounding. Passion, not Bond villain.

b Cite bogus statistics. "Hallmark cleared three billion dollars last February alone." "Every Valentine's Day, American women gain on average 1.6 pounds from consuming candy hearts, boxes of chocolate, and love-themed treats." Statistics sound like you've done research. Research gives your argument credence.

c Give her an out. Let your girlfriend know that you don't need a day to tell you when she's special. Every day is Valentine's Day, as far as you're concerned. You just want to hang out. Together. This lets her feel good about not having a traditional Valentine's Day. (It also leaves the door open for her to get you a gift.)

② Death Takes Out a Holiday

Is your girlfriend the sweet, sentimental type? Then this is the method you should try. Pick a pet from your past that died a long time ago. Or better yet, make one up. It can be a dog, cat, hamster, or any fuzzy mammal.

WARNING
When selecting a long-lost pet, no reptiles. Dead snakes get as much sympathy as child abusers. Plus, it's a pretty freaky pet, you weirdo.

When the time comes to talk about Valentine's Day, be emotionally distant. Because your girlfriend wants to know everything about your life, she'll ask you what's going on. That's when you drop the dead-pet bomb. "Sparky died on Valentine's Day. I know it's crazy and I should have recovered after all these years but . . ." It's not a happy holiday for you. You think of him every year. He was your best friend. "Now, if you absolutely must, have-to, gonna-die-if-you-don't, we can still go out and have dinner. I'd just rather not." This will get you dead-pet sympathy points in addition to relinquishing you from any Valentine's-related obligations.

FIDO
Chased his
last car
Feb. 14, 2000

**"He's never dead, Steve,
as long as you remember him."**

Pulling Her Heartstrings:
How to Look Emotionally Distant

a Wear the weight of the world by looking generally disheveled. Put on a wrinkled shirt, don't shave or comb your hair. (Maintain your regular bathing and tooth-brushing habits; no need to overdo it.)

b Practice your sad puppy-dog stare in the mirror. When mention of the day in question arises, assume this expression and let your sentences trail off when you speak.

C Sneak a snack in before dinner, then eat nothing while at the table. Instead, pick at your food and spell mournful messages with your green beans.

Overachieving at Underperforming

If you have the foresight and resources, a few weeks before Valentine's Day, place a childhood photo of yourself and your alleged pet someplace where your girlfriend will come across it. Keep in mind that the pet needn't actually have been yours—in fact, feel free to forge the whole scene using a picture of a dog cut out from a magazine and an old family snapshot. Combine these with a computer, a scanner, and some rudimentary photo-manipulation software and anyone can craft a heartbreaking scene from yesteryear. The point is, you're alongside your "pet" looking young, sensitive, and vulnerable. And when your girlfriend inquires, say tersely, "Oh, that's me and . . . Sparky." Then pause for effect and immediately change the subject. She'll remember.

③ Playing the Ex Card

Is your girlfriend the jealous type? Then this should end your Valentine's woes. You see, women hate when you talk about your ex-girlfriends. They absolutely despise it. And comparing your girlfriend to your ex is usually a big no-no. Use that to your advantage. All you have to do is let her know that Valentine's Day reminds you of Miss Ex and how much she loved every aspect of the holiday. The teddy bears, the chocolates, the card that says "Be Mine." Every time you see anything Valentine's-related, you think of how shallow she was. Your girl will do backflips to rid the world of everything red, white, and pink. The money you save on roses alone will fuel your bar tab for months.

If you have to get her something on Valentine's Day, lingerie is the way to go. It's a completely acceptable gift that's not really for her.

Chapter 32

Negotiating Anniversaries: Dodging Milestones

Everyone loves to celebrate milestones: your first steps, your first words, the first time you wrote your name in the snow. But women tend to go overboard. Has a woman ever said to you, "Oh my God, it's been exactly ten days since we first kissed." These completely arbitrary celebrations of meaningless dates can drive you mad. You must nip her time-obsessed clock-watching in the bud.

When she starts droning on about your one-month anniversary, explain to her that you'd rather not celebrate it. In fact, you prefer no mention of months two through eleven. When she responds with sadness, anger, or disbelief, you tell her, "No, no, you misunderstand. I don't celebrate these minor milestones, but it's not because they aren't special. It's because I want this relationship to last a very long time, and we shouldn't say, 'Yeah! We made it to month three.' Instead, we should know we're gonna make it. And this will make the real anniversaries that much more special—like our first year together.

Trust me, fellas, this works. She'll probably still try to pull some stuff at month six, but gently remind her that half a year is the lifespan of a blue jay—too short to celebrate. It's not true, but confusing poetics usually changes the subject.

Any anniversary with a zero on the end of it is very important. Any anniversary with a five on the end of it is mildly important. Any anniversary with "month" in it better be referring to a baby's age.

When the big anniversaries do come up, you must remember them. Put it in your calendar, write it on the fridge, tell your mom—whatever you need to do to be reminded. You cannot forget. She won't. And if you do, you'll betray your whole only-the-big-anniversaries system, and you'll soon be as unhappy as she is.

On the special day, take her to the restaurant or hot dog stand that you went to on your first date.

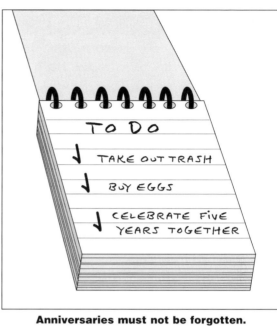

**Anniversaries must not be forgotten.
Remind yourself any way you can.**

This simple gesture says: Aww, he remembers. Can you believe that memory alone gets you points? It's amazing but true. So write that down too.

After dinner, take her on a walk, and tell her that you've never been happier than this past ___ year(s) and that you only pray you're half as happy the next year. Come upon a tree where you have precarved a heart around both your initials. This ridiculous and free gesture is the cherry on her perfect evening. After that she'll give you her kidney if you ask for it.

Chapter 33

Event Stacking:
1 + 1 = 1

Do you know a guy whose birthday happens to land on Christmas? Sucks for him—he never gets his own day. No one bothers to get him two gifts, no one's in town to celebrate with him, and no matter how famous he gets, he's never going to get a holiday named after himself. You can't trump Jesus.

This knowledge can help you with special events in your relationship. It's called event stacking, and it's a simple concept: By squeezing two holidays or special events into one celebration, you minimize the gifting and the money spent. You're killing two birds with one present. If you met your girlfriend around Valentine's Day, make that your anniversary. If her birthday is near the holidays, make it a Very Special Christmas. For event stacking to work, you need good timing and a lot of luck. But in the end, it's really about the money you save. Those piles and piles of money.

Chapter 34

I Made It Myself:
The Homemade Gift

Every woman wants to feel special, and if your girlfriend gets something no other woman on Earth has, she knows she's a one-of-a-kind lady. Who cares if it cost three bucks and it's mostly old popsicle sticks? You made it just for her.

Here is where the master craftsman comes in. There are two main items you can create that are acceptable homemade gifts: a piece of art or a poem.

Art doesn't generally have to be very good. In fact, if it's terrible, she'll get misty and emotional at the fact that you accepted the challenge of doing some-thing new and different despite your obvi-ous lack of artistic skill. So make it suck! Just slap some paint on a canvas, sign it, and have it framed. A good frame can turn any piece of crap into high art. There's probably a discount framing shop near you where you can frame it yourself on the cheap. Remember, a smaller canvas means less to paint and less to pay for the frame. And small is "cute."

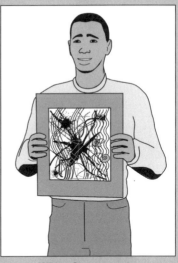

When it comes to homemade gifts, art generally doesn't have to be very good.

And now the art of wordsmithery. Don't be afraid of poetry, no matter how bad your grades were in English class. It's quick, it's easy, and if you do it right, it's like Spanish fly.

The Perfect Poem

- Don't even think about starting with "Roses are red." It's old, sad, and shows you don't care.

- Start with a simple A-B-A-B rhyme scheme. That just means every other line must rhyme.

- Use her name in the text. Personalizing the poem makes it special.

- Write it out neatly on a clean sheet of paper. Use colored ink and add big pretentious flourishes to your lettering.

- Put a date on it, sign it, and carefully put it in a cologne-scented envelope. As any good chef will tell you, presentation is 90 percent of the meal.

WARNING

One option—a risky one—is to copy an old poem. Your girlfriend probably isn't writing a thesis on Shakespearean love sonnets, but cribbing from a master poet has its downsides—there is always a chance you'll be caught. Nothing's more pathetic than a plagiarized poem. On the upside, the fact remains that somebody probably said it first and said it best. So if you're gonna steal, steal from Wordsworth, Byron, or Yeats. They've written extensively on the subject of love, yearning, and desire. Just make sure you modernize the old English terminology. Otherwise, your wench may thinketh you foolsbane.

Chapter 35
Getting Yours

Congratulations! With your newfound knowledge you should be able to survive every holiday and observance. As a lucky bonus, gift-giving is a two-way street. You get a gift too. Here's how to get what you want:

1 Drop Hints

This is the easiest, most direct way. And unlike you, women listen. "I would love season tickets to the local sports team." "I would love a sixty-inch Sony plasma screen TV." "I would love to bring another woman into our bedroom." Obviously you must find something within her price range and moral values.

2 Buy It Yourself

Buy something you really want, then sheepishly return it, claiming it's too frivolous. "I can't buy this for myself. It's something I want, not something I need." If you look sad enough when returning it, she should get the hint.

3 Take the Gift Back

When she gives you a gift, she expects you to like it. You don't have to. Explain to her that it isn't exactly what you wanted. It's great, but it's just not you. Wouldn't she be happier if you got exactly what you wanted? Her disappointment will be focused on why she didn't know you well enough, not on your being an ingrate.

Section IX
Her Parents

Unless your girlfriend is a robot you created in your basement/laboratory, she probably has parents. It's an evolutionary inevitability. People need parents— or some reasonable facsimile. Without parents, who would buy those XXL Hawaiian shirts or the acid washed jeans with the elastic waistband? Your girlfriend probably has somewhere around two parents: a mother and a father. And it's important that they like you. If you're mean or apathetic toward them, they can subtly urge their daughter to dump you, which she may choose to do. Or, worse, she could rebel against their advice and push herself closer to you. You must find a careful balance, one wherein her folks love you but, at the same time, you maintain little contact with them. With a bit of help, those uncomfortable dinners at the Olive Garden can be a thing of the past.

Chapter 36
Pleased Not to Meet You

Your first step is to avoid ever making contact with her parents. Unless they're college professors who teach courses on modern culture, they're more than likely boring older people with whom you have little in common. They probably have simple lives, but complex, long-winded ways to tell stories about those lives. And unless you love tales about how the rental car isn't a full-size like they wanted, or how much a gallon of milk used to cost back when people were decent to one another, you probably want to avoid her parents.

How to avoid her parents:

1 Be Out When They're In

Find out when they're going to be in town and plan a mini vacation. You don't have to go far, just out of visiting range.

2 Miss Them by Seconds

When they're in town, stake out your girlfriend's house and wait until they leave before you come in. When your girlfriend tells you that you just missed them, be upset and exclaim, "Darn the luck!"

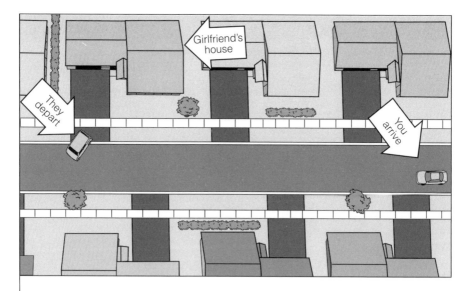

③ Be Contagious

You would love to meet them, but unfortunately you have some temporary illness that could wreak havoc upon their aging, brittle bones and fragile immune systems. It's best if you stay quarantined on the couch.

How to still make them love you:

① Send Them a Bottle

After you feign illness so you can avoid that meet-the-boyfriend dinner, find out where they're eating and send over a bottle of wine. It's cheap, it's easy, and it's classy. It says, "Sorry I missed you, but I'm really a good guy. Get sorta drunk on me."

② Get Them Tickets to a Show

It doesn't matter if it's a matinee for a middle school talent show or first-row opening night on Broadway. Almost any tickets to any show will do. Just make sure it's something unadventurous and safe, like Jay Leno or community theater.

❸ Put Together a To-Do Kit

Go to the nearest hotel and grab brochures for every vineyard, golf course, and walking tour in town. Talk to the concierge/front desk goon and ask what would be fun for old people to do. Plan out a day of activities to fill their time. Present them with all these options and they will think you're thoughtful and kind. When they ask you to tag along, you can beg off: "I'm so sorry, I would love to visit that gorge, but I have work to do." (Showing up dressed for work will go a long way toward selling this one.) Her folks will think you're sweet and a solid provider because your career is important to you. And once they're off on their excursion, you're free to laze around in your underwear for the rest of the day.

"I'd love to visit that gorge with you, but look at me, I'm off to work."

Chapter 37

"Such a Nice Boy!"

Since you can't run forever, eventually you must face her folks. And when you do, you should definitely be prepared. Before you meet the parents for the first time, there are a few rules you should familiarize yourself with.

1 Look Nice

This means wear clean clothes, groom yourself, and don't wear your old high school basketball T-shirt with the holes in it. In fact, throw that away—your nipple's showing.

2 Be Polite

Don't assume that you can call them by their first names. Say "Mr." or "Mrs." and "Ma'am" or "Sir." Use "thank yous" and "pleases." And never swear. It's amazing how genteel and refined you'll sound when you refrain from saying "bootylicious."

3 Don't Talk Too Much

If you say nothing, you can't accidentally insult them or prove what an idiot you are. If you babble on and on, it reveals too much about yourself, and they might piece together what you're really like.

4 Don't Get Drunk

This may be difficult, but try, dammit. Alcohol impairs judgment and motor skills and causes one to talk too much. See above.

5 Be Prepared for Their Questions

"Where are you from? Where did you go to school? What do you do? Why are you staring at my wife's chest?" Clever, preplanned answers make you seem on the ball and witty.

6 Don't Get Too Touchy with Their Angel

Groping their baby is a bad idea. A simple kiss hello will suffice. Maybe some hand-holding (if you can stand it). That's it. Parents don't like to think of their offspring as sexual beings. If her dad sees you slipping her the tongue, something innate will take over his mind and he'll want to kill you. So don't let him feel uncomfortable. Let him know that you care about her, but that you've definitely, 100 percent never seen her in Little Bo Peep lingerie crawling across your bed to get a spanking. It might miff him a little to think about that.

7 Give Them a Good "Good Night"

Tell them that you were very pleased to meet them and that you can see where your girlfriend gets her good looks and strong morals. Or some such drivel. This flatters them and subtly reaffirms that you're not sleeping with her, because moral people do not do that out of wedlock.

Chapter 38

Connecting with Her Dad

Despite your attempts at play-acting and diversion, there's still a good chance that her old man knows the score. He knows what it's like to be in your position, and he knows how you think. This doesn't mean he (necessarily) wants to rip your arms off. He just wants to make sure the guy dating his daughter isn't the biggest sex freak on the planet. Your job is to put him at ease. Make him feel that you're one of the few decent fellows left on the planet. Take advantage of the fact that he wants to believe you're the clumsy, naïve boy who prefers holding hands and occasionally fumbles his way through necking at the drive-in. "Golly, Betty Lou, I respect you. Let's continue kissing, but remember, the tongue is the devil's whip."

"Hey, my favorite team is the Tigers!"

"Really? I had no idea!"

If he's too smart for that, your last hope is to try to connect with him in a meaningful way. If he likes you, maybe he won't wish for your death upon sight. Here are a few ways to bond with her dad:

1 Know a Little About His Favorite Team

Find out from your girlfriend what his favorite sports team is. Do a little research and be able to discuss their best player, a famous game that you "saw," and several talking points on how you think they can improve next season. Nothing manufactures superficial camaraderie better than a shared affinity for a sports franchise.

WARNING

Make sure you're not a fan of his team's biggest rival. If you are, keep it a secret. It just makes life easier if you don't have a hat with the mascot that he's been trained to hate.

Overachieving at Underperforming

If you're truly ambitious and prepared to commit to an allegiance that you may need to maintain for the rest of your life (or at least until your future father-in-law dies, if it comes to that), consider adopting as your favorite team one that is the archrival of his. This can engender a good-natured rivalry that will become the predominant topic of conversation whenever you come into contact with your girlfriend's dad, distracting him from your many true flaws. And if you really want to maximize the benefits of this tactic, choose an archrival that his team consistently thrashes. He'll find you pathetic and less threatening as a result.

② Partake in His Hobby

Hopefully it will be golf or beer-can collecting. But even if it's wood-working, feign interest and ask questions. This master-apprentice relationship allows him to feel good about passing along valuable skills or information.

③ Make Fun of a Politician Whom He Hates

Connecting politically means you share the same values and ideals.

Never use his first name, even if he demands it. Call him "Mr." and then his last name. It's a sign of respect and he'll appreciate it. And never call him "Dad," even in jest. He hates that.

④ Buy Him a Beer

Take him to your local watering hole and buy him a cold one. It shows him that he's young enough to hang with the guys, and that you're old enough to be a man. Also, make sure you drink what he's drinking. Mimicry is the sincerest form of flattery.

Chapter 39

Prince-Charming Her Mom

Her mother's usually a little easier to deal with than her father. She just wants to see her baby happy. Many moms don't care if you have face tattoos, a cache of guns, or a prison record, as long as you're good to her daughter. There are a few things you can do to make Mom work for you.

1 Fear of No Grandchildren

Just the idea of a grandbaby is enough to drive her mother into fits of delight. Let her mom see you playing with a group of kids at the park, making faces at the toddler in the booth next to you at lunch, or show-

**Pretend that you like children. Your girlfriend's
mom will see you as a potential grandchild producer
and will make sure that you're kept happy.**

ing off photos of nieces and nephews. Then casually mention that you really love kids and want to have many of them. She will envision her late years populated by attentive grandchildren doting on her while she sews booties and puts together scrapbooks of the family's memories. After that, she'll pressure your girlfriend into keeping you happy.

2 Compliment Her

Women of a certain age tend to obsess about how they're not exactly a size four anymore. A simple "Did you lose weight? Because you look terrific. I'm serious" will bump you from bozo to keeper in her book. You can also drop ten years from her age, and act shocked when she corrects you. Buttering her up makes her happy. And it ups your Christmas gift. You just went from sweater to MP3 player.

3 Include Her in Your Plans

It's inevitable that you're going to have to spend time with her mother, so why not take charge and make the most out of a bad situation? If she's in town and you and your girlfriend are making plans for yourselves, ask her to join you. When she does tag along, make sure she finds out that it was your idea. She'll think of you as a considerate young man who enjoys her company. And, as a bonus, she'll foot the bill most of the time.

4 Buy Her Some Fancy Moisturizer

Plunk down twenty bucks and get her some overpriced department store skin lotion. It's a little gift that she'll use occasionally and that will remind her of your generosity. Just make sure it doesn't say "anti-aging" anywhere on it. You don't want to send the message that you think she's a wrinkly old hag, even if she is.

Section X
Fighting

Historians believe the first fight between a man and a woman was between Ug the Caveman and his sometime girlfriend, Booga Booga. She wanted to go check out this new thing called fire down at the Neanderthal place, but he wanted to watch the game (some elk). She grunted that it had been an ice age since he took her anywhere, and that he should evolve already. Ug couldn't grasp the idea of a wheel, but he did know unreasonable when he heard it. After a screaming match, Ug ended up sleeping on the less comfortable slab of rock in the den.

Fighting has been around for a long time, and men have been losing for thousands of years. Since we can't club women over the head anymore, we have to figure out other ways of dealing with them.

Chapter 40

Don't Take the Bait: Avoidance Techniques

Think of the old master teaching the reckless young warrior in a kung fu movie. He trains him on the skills to win any fight, but warns him to use them only as a last resort. Avoiding the battle is always better. You can't lose a fight you're not in.

Here are some avoidance techniques that should help you stay out of the fray:

1 Pick Your Battles

Ask yourself if the fight is worth it. Do you really care that you're right and she's wrong? What do you have to gain by winning this fight? Can it be stopped or are you already committed to playing it out? If winning is meaningless, don't start the fight.

② Don't Be Stubborn

Are you completely wrong, know it, and just fighting out of some stubborn, macho need to win no matter how ridiculously wrong you are? Stop and think about how stupid that is. Concede the point before it escalates. It's easier to eat crow when it's warm.

Stop a fight early and admit you're wrong. It's easier to eat crow when it's warm.

③ Take Her Side

There is no fight if there is no one to fight with. If she's mad at you because you left your underwear on the kitchen floor, agree with her that it was foolish and must never happen again. If she calls you names, then you call yourself worse names. She will have nowhere to go, become bewildered, and give up.

④ Vanish

Go somewhere else. She cannot fight with someone who isn't there. This is only a temporary solution, as women tend to dwell on things and can jump right back into an argument without missing a beat even after a two-year absence. So use that time to prepare a new tack to use upon your return. If you return.

Any captain of a high school debate team knows that the key to a suc-cessful argument is stating your position in a clear and concise manner while refuting any points your opponent may have. Thank you, Captain Nerd. But what if you're the one who's wrong? What if logic and reason are your enemies? Or what if your girlfriend is the stubborn one and says something like, "I just feel the way I feel and there's nothing that will change my mind"? In order to win any fight, the Overachieving Underperformer must use the tools available to him: distraction, denial and reversal.

① Distraction

During a round of golf, talking in the middle of your buddy's backswing will probably put his drive off the fairway and into the rough. Diverting your girlfriend's attention from the original focus of the fight achieves the same effect—except she won't toss your pitching wedge into the nearest water hazard.

One way to distract her is to pick another fight. This may seem counterintuitive, but it's not. This, in effect, changes the topic of conversation to a more manageable fight. Try saying something like, "Oh yeah? Well, I don't like your sister." This pushes her off into another rant, one that is more controllable or that you have prepared for in advance. Just make sure you go from a large argument to a small one, not the other way around. If you're fighting about leaving the empty milk carton in the fridge, don't bring up how you wish she would drop that fifteen pounds she once claimed she "could lose if she really wanted to." That's a distraction you don't want.

A second method of distraction is changing the subject from the bone of contention to another, tangentially related but entirely inarguable topic. If she's fighting with you for being arrested for public intoxication, divert her from the argument by telling her that if you had the chance to do it all over again, you wouldn't change a thing. You would much rather stumble home on foot than try to drive drunk. It doesn't matter that you don't

"Look over there."

have a car or that you were arrested during a Mardi Gras party outside your house. Changing the subject with righteous indignation can end most fights.

❷ Denial

Lawyers call it plausible deniability. When it benefits a client to "not know" certain facts, and when there is no definitive way to prove whether the client has that knowledge, he claims deniability.

The burden of proof is on your girlfriend. If she has no hard evidence that you went to that strip club, it is deniable. Just repeat over and over that she is wrong and it didn't happen. Stick to your guns and give no ground.

"It wasn't me."

Sometimes your denial doesn't even have to be plausible. If you made out with Tyra Banks in front of hundreds of witnesses, and there's video documentation, and you signed an admission of guilt and you're wearing a shirt that says "I made out with Tyra Banks and all I got was this lousy T-shirt," you can still deny it. Vehement denial plants a seed of doubt in your girlfriend's mind. Nurture that seed with constant "It wasn't me's." She really wants to believe there is an evil twin out there trying to ruin your life. Help her.

❸ Reversal

It's not just for vasectomies anymore. Reversal is the sudden flipping of a quarrel to focus on a fault you find in her—in effect, blaming her for your actions.

For example, if she's upset you went to a strip club, you can blame her for driving you to go there. "I only went to that filthy place because I was feeling lonely and sexually frustrated. I would much rather see you in sexy lingerie strutting your stuff than some skank I have no feelings for. If you're willing . . . I bought this French maid costume. I think you'll find it's perfectly tailored to fit your body. P.S. You're welcome."

If you left the kitchen a mess: "You're never satisfied with me. How can I ever please you? Plus, you never praise me when I do something good. Why do I even bother?"

If she finds a girl's phone number in your jeans: "Yeah, well, I never get jealous when you're talking to this Mike character who you claim is your boss. I heard you talking to him the other day about 'scheduling.' What does that even mean? Are you cheating on me?"

"It was you."

A careful combination of all three tactics should get you the desired result: a W in the argument column.

Chick Tricks

Tears: Your Secret Weapon

One surefire way to halt an argument is to start crying. Crying is almost second nature to women. They'll turn on the waterworks for almost anything: a broken nail, a run in their pantyhose, when the chef puts dressing on her salad after she specifically asked for it on the side. It's madness.

Men, on the other hand, rarely cry. Only when he has to put his dog down, or if his team loses the pennant, does society deem it an acceptable time for a man to weep. So women will be shocked when you whip out the tears during a fight.

A carefully timed sob will unnerve your girlfriend—women are so unaccustomed to seeing a man cry that they'll think whatever brought on the boo-hoos must be an incredibly huge deal. She'll assume she touched upon something deep and sensitive, an area you've always kept hidden but are now sharing with her. This will cause her to become sympathetic and slip into automatic "mommy" mode. "There, there, I don't care if you kicked my cat. He was probably asking for it."

So when the time comes, squirt a few. But be careful not to overdo it—you don't want to come across as a pathetic emotional wreck. Consider bawling like a little girl only when an argument is spinning out of control and you have no way of winning it. Resorting to heaving, hysterical sobs is your last lifeboat, so use it wisely.

Chapter 42

The Benefits of Losing Outright

In 1919 the Chicago White Sox threw the World Series, thereby earning the moniker "Black Sox" and tarnishing a wholesome sport that would later be tarnished by segregation, sex scandals, steroid use, and the designated hitter. Fueled by greed and "Shoeless" Joe Jackson's need for soft, deep pile carpet, the once beloved team was universally reviled and thrown out of baseball in disgrace. Unlike the Black Sox, losing on purpose to your girlfriend can be a good thing. Winning gives her a sense of triumph, and you're the only one who has to know it's all a sham.

The Seven Benefits of Highly Effective Losing:

- When you take the blame for something small, it builds "honesty" credit that can be cashed in later. "I always admit when I'm wrong—why are you doubting me when I say that the bra in my backseat is clearly from a home-less woman who broke in, hated her uncomfortable black lace 34D demicups, and flung them carelessly to the floor before departing in a huff?"

- Women will genuinely be surprised if you take the loss well. They'll think that you don't have any antiquated macho resentment, and that you therefore accept that women are equal to men. Stupid broads.

- Time saved not yelling translates into time available for beer pong.

- Celebrating her win at your favorite ribs joint.

- Sex is not cut off for a month.

- Don't have to sleep on couch.

- You know that you let her win, which means she didn't really win at all!

It's a hard lesson to learn, but losing is a winning strategy.

Section XI
The Vacation

Ironically, vacationing can be stressful. There's planning, booking, packing, traveling, and forgetting you left the iron on. Okay, so you've never used the iron, but you get the idea. Taking a vacation isn't all mini liquor bottles and water parks. The last thing you want to worry about, on top of everything else, is keeping your girlfriend happy. But the Overachieving Underperformer knows methods to make any trip as smooth as the sunscreen she'll be rubbing onto your back.

Chapter 43

Getting Her Involved

If you want your holiday to be enjoyable, you have to get your girlfriend involved. But you don't want her making the decision on where you'll be going. She'll choose a quaint bed-and-breakfast where you can go on nature walks. So if you don't want her pointing out local flora and fauna, explain to your girlfriend that you're going on vacation, and would love if she came. This makes it your vacation, not hers. She'll be so smitten with you because you included her, she won't even care where you're going, be it Las Vegas, the Baseball Hall of Fame, or a barbecue tour of the Southwest.

After choosing the destination, you must keep her involved in the planning. Here's a list of a few things to make her think she was an integral part of Team Vacation.

1 Transportation

Let her pick the means to get there. Whether you're flying, cruising, or taking the train, let her book it. This saves you the hassle, and she is to blame if things go wrong. (Exception: If you're driving, don't let her navigate. That's not involvement, that's just stupidity.)

2 Lodging

Let her pick the hotel. This will make her happy. Just make sure you tell her what amenities the place must have—high definition TV with the optional sports package, or high definition TV with the optional adult package.

WARNING

Make sure your girlfriend knows your budget before she makes any reservations. Left to her own devices, you'll be paying through the nose for the privilege of sleeping in a room with two couches and a breakfast nook.

---

3 Food

Let her pick out where you eat. For your girlfriend, it's all about sampling the local cuisine, so indulge her. You can find something palatable on most any menu. Steak is steak—unless you're in India. But what the hell are you doing in India?

If you keep her involved, it'll keep her busy, and she will think it's her vacation too.

**Keep her involved in the decision-making process
and she'll think it was all her idea.**

For those of you who like easy-to-read graphic representations, you'll love this handy chart. It gives the pros and cons of various vacation destinations to help you decide where best to take your better half. For those of you who hate easy-to-read charts, I'm sorry, but this book is nonrefundable.

Destination	Pros	Cons
The Beach	• Warm • Cheap • Bikini-clad women surrounding you	• Sharks • Fat and/or hairy people with no shame • Girlfriend won't let you enjoy bikini-clad women
The Mountains	• Breathtaking views • Adorable girl teaching you to snowboard • Post-slopes hot-tubbing	• Cold • Potentially debilitating skiing accidents • Avalanche!!! • Carrying your girlfriend's boots, skis, and poles the six miles to the car
Europe	• Cultural mecca • Women with cool accents • Can blame anything on the Germans • Photo of you giving the Mona Lisa the finger	• Figuring out confusing money conversions • Don't know if French guy is making fun of you • Girlfriend might think you're going to pop the question

Destination	Pros	Cons
Canada	• A hockey game on every corner • National drink: maple syrup • Socialized health care allows you to feel immortal	• Exotic as a hangnail • Average temperature: 2 • The word is "about," not "aboot." • Girlfriend thinks you're too cheap to take her to a real country
Australia	• Great Barrier Reef • Sydney Opera House • Watching the water swirl down the drain the other way	• Boomerang to the face • Vegemite anything • Girlfriend falls for young Mel Gibson look-alike and goes on walkabout with him
Cruise	• The splendor of the briny deep • Shrimp cocktail at every meal	• Seasickness • Giant squid attack • Shuffleboard elbow • People who like cruises • Nowhere to storm off to after fight with girlfriend
Camping	• Communing with nature • Campfire stories • S'mores • Cuddling in sleeping bags	• Bugs • Stomping grounds for movie serial killers • Have to crap in woods • Girlfriend turns two-man tent into one-woman/ half-a-man tent
Wine Country	• None	• My God, man, get out of there!

Chapter 44

Around the World on 80 Bucks: Vacations on a Budget

Do you "summer" in a different place from where you "winter"? Have you ever shipped your horse anywhere? Do you have no idea what Windex is for? Do you have anyone in your employ named "Jeeves"? If you answered yes to any of these questions, then this chapter is not for you, Lord Moneybags.

For the rest of us, we know that traveling can be ridiculously expensive—doubly so when your girlfriend wants to stop at every bauble shop in Paris. The Overachieving Underperformer can easily curb his spending while on vacation with his woman. Here is a handy travel list for a man vacationing on the cheap.

1 Motel Not Hotel

It's just a bed, so why not go cheap? If your girlfriend complains, tell her this wasn't what you thought it was going to be. The Web site made it look better. Also, you didn't come all the way to England just to sit around in a hotel room. It's just a place to sleep. Now let's go look at that Stonehenge.

2 Ask the Locals

Locals know the best deals on places to eat, sleep, and shop. So ask them. But don't do it in front of your girlfriend. She should think you found this charming bistro on your own and—what do you know—it's inexpensive!

3 Bar the Minibar

It doesn't matter how starving or thirsty your girlfriend is, never let her eat the seven-dollar Kit-Kat or drink the nine-dollar Diet Coke. They aren't worth it. Save a fortune and think ahead.

4 Drive

Instead of tossing down a fortune on airfare, get in the car. It's cheaper, there are no airport headaches and delays, and you set your own schedule. A good cutoff point is six hours. Most men will not want to sit in a confined space with their girlfriend longer than that. Better make that four hours.

5 Don't Shop

Your girlfriend wants a souvenir? Get her a snow globe. Or better yet, steal a towel. If she wants to shop on her own, let her—with her own money. Buying crap just because it says "Cancun" on it is absurd.

Chapter 45

Separate Vacations:
The Holy Grail

Some of the greatest writers in the world have written travelogues about their journeys through the dense jungles of Borneo, across the sandy dunes of the Kalahari Desert, or touching the ceiling of the world in the

Question: What's not in this picture of two traveling pioneers?
Answer: A girlfriend.

Himalayan Mountains of Nepal. What do all these legendary globe-trotters have in common? They left their girlfriends at home.

No one has ever read about the expedition of Lewis and Clark and Clark's girl, Lindsay. The true Overachieving Underperformer will turn a regular vacation into a vacation from his girlfriend. Here are a few ways you can do this.

① Too Busy

Plan it opposite her busiest time at work or during one of her business trips. Just tell her it's the only time you could get off. You're upset that you have to spend the week partying with seven of your best friends in sunny Ibiza. But you'll have to make do without her.

② Costs Too Much

Make it too expensive for her. Estimate her share of the trip at a small fortune. Just fudge the numbers enough to where she will say no. Overestimate the cost of the flight, hotel, food, and incidentals. The key here is getting her to say no, so you must not waver on your feigned willingness to go together.

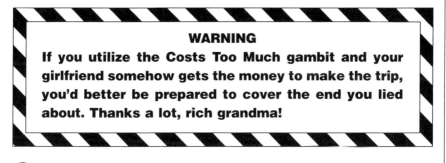

WARNING
If you utilize the Costs Too Much gambit and your girlfriend somehow gets the money to make the trip, you'd better be prepared to cover the end you lied about. Thanks a lot, rich grandma!

③ Buddy Wins Free Trip for Two!

And he picked you to go with him. This is a lie, but it's simple and she can't complain.

Overachieving at Underperforming

We've all experienced a sudden urge to get away from it all. The hustle and bustle of life becomes too much for us, and we must give in to our wanderlust. ROAD TRIP! Road trips are usually spur-of-the-moment vacations that don't allow the time necessary for laying the groundwork to keep your girlfriend from tagging along. This is when you should consider employing the ultimate risk-taker's maneuver: the Disappear.

This method requires no advance planning and is simple to execute. You just leave. Once on your way, you make one simple phone call to your girlfriend, timed so as to ensure that her voice mail picks it up. Explain that a sudden trip arose and you realized it would be a good opportunity to "clear your head." You're sorry that you didn't know about it sooner and that the sudden notice has made it impossible for you to bring her along. Give her a rough idea of when you'll be back, and promise to call her immediately upon your return. Then turn off your phone and enjoy.

Make no mistake about it: You will be in the doghouse after this one. But the beauty of the Disappear is its honesty. When her barrage of criticism is unleashed upon your return, point out that you called her as soon as you were under way, and you called only her, because she means more to you than anyone else. You don't want to be the type of friend who abandons his buddies once he meets Miss Special, and you're struggling to balance your boyish spontaneity with your desire to be the guy she deserves. Abandoning her was nothing personal. If she continues to rail at you, pull out your secret weapon: the gift. A tank top from whichever oasis you decided to escape to. Make sure you get it one size too small. "You're not an extra small? Could've fooled me."

Section XII
Love

What hasn't been said about love? It makes men dive in front of bullets. It keeps songwriters and poets out of debt. In sci-fi movies when you ask evil computers to define it, they are so confounded that they explode.

The Overachieving Underperformer knows that love can be a wonderful thing. But he also understands that sometimes love makes people do crazy things, and he exploits this knowledge. When you're in love, the OU maxim is simple: Minimize your stupidity, and maximize your enjoyment.

Chapter 46
Recognizing the Signs

Okay, so you think you're in love, but you're not sure. Most people say that if you don't know, then you're not. But sometimes you can't see the forest for the trees. Here are a few signs to assist you in recognizing love.

1 Idiocy

Are you using baby talk when on the phone with her? Are you making kissy faces at her over dinner? Do you hold hands and frolic in public? Do you not care what other people think of the both of you? You may be in love.

2 Free Flow of Money

When you stop caring how much money you're spending on her, it's a good signal you're in love. A man in lust will do the same thing, but only to a point. A man in love will buy his girlfriend things beyond all reason, even if he can't afford it.

3 Appearance

Have you become more fastidious about your appearance? Do you look different than before you met her? Are you wearing a shirt she bought you right now? Sometimes love makes us do stupid things, like dress how she wants us to dress instead of how we feel comfortable. If you're a T-shirt and jeans guy and suddenly you're wearing khakis and oxfords, you may have been bitten by the love bug.

④ Listening

Are you not only hearing every word she says, but thoughtfully taking it all in, i.e., "listening"? Your patient attention may just be love. What about the details of her life? Do you know her size in everything (including ring)? Her favorite color? The brand name of the bread she loves? The names of her best friend's cats? That's love, pal.

⑤ Other Women Are Invisible

Did that hot assistant in your office fall off your radar? When you go out drinking and meet a group of girls, do you immediately tell them you have a girlfriend? Do you think strip clubs are a waste of money? Welcome to Lovetown.

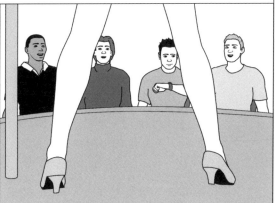

Have you lost all interest in other women? You may be in love.

WARNING
Never fall in love with her sister, her best friend, or the girl across the street. Your life is not like a movie, and your hapless attempts to make it so will end badly, maybe with a knife in your chest.

Chapter 47

Better Left Unsaid:
Avoiding the L-Word

If you don't want to tell your girlfriend you love her, the best way to avoid using the L word is never to hear it from her lips. If she never says it, you never have to reciprocate. So avoid conversations about your feelings, or the dreaded define-the-relationship talk. Tell her you're having tons of fun with her, you like her a lot, and you don't want to screw things up with unnecessary labels. This should buy you some time to either run for the hills or suck it up and let love rule.

The love you/like you scenario can lead to hurt feelings, anger, resentment, and an overall feeling of foolishness. So if she does throw out the L-word, you need to make a decision. Do you return fire? Or do you give her a "Well, I like you a lot too"?

If you choose not to reciprocate, you'd better be prepared for dire consequences. She put her heart on the line and you pushed it away. Too many lonely bachelor pads are maintained by men who "liked" their girlfriends. A much better option is to just say the words "I love you too, baby." She'll be

Love is everywhere. Demystify the term.

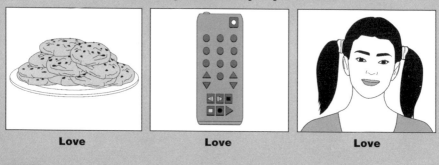

Love   Love   Love

happy, and you don't have to mean it. For example, when you say you love brownies, it's true, but not in the romantic sense. The same can go for your girlfriend. You can define love any way you want. Plus, you're not really hurting her because there is always a possibility that you could learn to genuinely love her—you could just be jumping the gun a little in saying so now.

Remember, no one can tell you what love means.

Chick Tricks

Taking the Love out of "Love"

The best way to take the power out of a word is to overuse it. Words once thought of as profane are now commonly used by third graders without turning a head. This principle doesn't just apply to obscenities. Consider taking the power out of the word "love" by introducing a new word: "krung."

This stroke of genius was developed by a legendary Overachieving Underperformer who prefers to remain anonymous. He had been dating a girl for only two months when she told him she loved him— and he quickly reciprocated.

His girlfriend was confused because he'd tossed the word back to her as if it were meaningless. When she questioned him about his casual usage, he explained: "Oh, I wasn't being casual. It's just that there is a greater love. A love that goes far beyond romantic or physical love. This super love is called krung. It can only be experienced when two people are so connected, so bonded, so perfectly in sync that their spirits intertwine. It may take years but I hope that someday we can be in krung. Until then, we should enjoy this love thing." After that, he could toss around "love" like it was a throw pillow.

Chapter 48

Making the Best of a Good Situation

So you freely admit that you're in love and, all in all, it's not a bad thing —now what could be wrong? It depends on who's doing what for whom.

Are you picking up her dry cleaning across town? Are you buying the groceries, unloading them, and cooking the meal? Are you washing her car? When you're in love, you do stupid things, and sometimes your lady will use your love to her advantage. The Overachieving Underperforming way is to reverse the curse: Flip the relationship around until she does more for you than you do for her.

1 Say No

Learn to say no to her requests. Make up an excuse or, better yet, just say you'd rather not. Either way, stand firm and nix any of her wishes that you find unreasonable. With time she'll grow to learn that you're not going to be sent on any frivolous errands, move any couches, or attend any poetry readings. If your girlfriend's of particularly stubborn stock, you may have to set your "I won't" sights a bit lower, but you'll still be better off than if you hadn't tried.

2 Be a Squeaky Wheel

Bug her about doing stuff for you. She will eventually tire of your nagging and do what you ask. It's a special favor to you. It would mean a lot. "I don't know why you can't do this one little thing for me." Thanks for the oil change, honey.

❸ Tradition

Turn certain nights into "traditions." If she cooks a meal, ask her to do it again the following week. Bam, it's a tradition: she cooks meatloaf every Wednesday. Try to turn Saturday into Do-Your-Laundry Day, and Monday into Buy-Your-Lunch Day. Get creative and make each tradition your own.

Before you know it, you'll be in the plus column of love-related chores.

Section XIII
Marriage

Most birds, especially penguins, parrots, geese, and cranes, choose one partner and mate for life. If their mate dies, they make no attempt to find another. Most mammals, on the other hand, tend toward promiscuity—spreading their seed to as many partners as possible to ensure the propagation of their genes.

Men are no different from our furry friends. Nature has ingrained in us the fear of settling down, and it's no small thing to overcome. We are constantly bombarded with negative images of marriage: a ball and chain, an old woman with her hair in curlers wielding a rolling pin and trailing seventy-five screaming kids. Add to this a fear of pedestrian (or nonexistent) sex and the skyrocketing divorce rate, and it's enough to make anyone run screaming for the hills at the mere mention of the word "marri-" . . . get back here.

Making the leap from having a girlfriend to having a wife is a difficult undertaking, but the Overachieving Underperformer carefully weighs every option and knows when to go for it and when to bail out of an inevitable nuptial Hindenburg.

Chapter 49

Delaying the Inevitable:
Rules of Nonengagement

If the thought of white gowns, bad toasts, and drunken uncles doing the chicken dance terrifies you, you're not alone. Marriage scares most young men. It's committing for the long haul, and giving up a part of your life that you secretly wish would never be over. For men who don't want to make that final leap: how do you avoid the subject of matrimony?

First, if you've only been dating a woman for a year or less, the subject of marriage shouldn't even come up. If it does, you should be worried. She may be husband hunting or looking for citizenship or she may even be a loon. Regardless, she's not someone you want to be spending your golden years with. Refer to Section XIV, on breaking up.

If a significant amount of time has passed in your relationship and you think she may be leaning toward the ultimate commitment, you must deal with it. You have to either avoid the conversation or convince her that marriage isn't right for you.

1 Avoiding the Conversation

Avoiding the conversation can be difficult. Everywhere she looks there are reminders of marriage, and she will try to broach the subject any way she can. Walk by a jewelry store, and she'll take a long look at the rings. Tell a seemingly innocent story about a friend of yours, and she'll dive in with, "Speaking of Mary . . ." Fill out her taxes, and she'll pipe in with, "You know what else would save a lot of money? That marriage deduction." You must tell her that you're not ready for that conversation just yet—but not to worry, you'll come to her and discuss it when the time is right. This will buy you some time, but eventually you may have to use the next tactic.

❷ Convincing Her That Marriage Isn't Right for You

You don't believe in marriage (at least not to her), so you have to make the case that it isn't all it's cracked up to be.

- "Do we really need a piece of paper to tell us that we're soul mates?" Why should a union be real because the state or some minister says so?

- Why do women define themselves as incomplete if they aren't married? "I think it's empowering if a woman is comfortably single."

- Marriage is just a legal bond created by society to reinforce old religious notions of women as property. "I respect you more than that."

- Ask her to point out one celebrity marriage that is perfect. If she gives an example, tell her he's gay and their marriage is a sham (which is probably true).

- The divorce rate is sky-high. In Western society today, marriage doesn't carry the same importance as it did during the 1950s. It's almost meaningless. "Who wants to enter into a contract that the general public has deemed dismissible? I'm glad we had this talk. See you after the game."

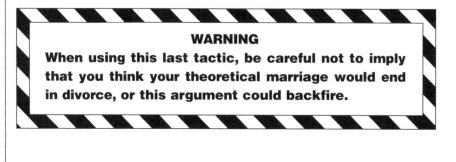

WARNING
When using this last tactic, be careful not to imply that you think your theoretical marriage would end in divorce, or this argument could backfire.

Chick Tricks

The Five Questions You Should Ask Yourself Before You Get Married

Before you put the barrel of the gun in your mouth, ask yourself five questions:

❶ Is She Attractive?

See Chapter 1 for why good looks are important. An ugly girl-friend is okay. It's not permanent. But an ugly wife? That's quite a commitment. Ask yourself: Would I feel proud introducing this woman as my wife?

❷ Can You Handle Her Family?

You don't marry just her, you marry her whole family. That means you inherit their problems, and your children, should you choose to have any, inherit her family's genetic makeup. Does her dad smell like broccoli? Does she have a brother with a heroin problem and a habit of "borrowing" jewelry? Is her mom going to move in after the old man dies?

❸ Will She Bear You Offspring?

You have to talk about children. Some women don't want children. Some men don't want children. Some women want ten kids. Some men want two. Some women can't have children. Some men can't have children. Discuss it before you tie the knot and learn she wants seventeen kids—all girls.

❹ Is She Financially Secure?

It's not just about how much money she has (though that is important). It's how responsible she is with the money she has.

If she's racked up huge debt and has eleven credit cards, she may not be "the one." In marriage, you incur all her debts and bad credit. So find that girl with the budget-management degree and daily fiscal calendar—she'll make sure you retire to an island, not some crappy apartment with no air-conditioning.

⑤ Do You Love Her?

Okay, this looks like an easy one. But there are many loveless marriages out there. Some people lie to themselves because they're convinced that marriage is the natural next step. Ask yourself if you truly, deeply love her. Would you dive in front of a bullet to save her? And ask yourself the reverse. Would she dive in front of a bullet for you? Love is a two-way street; both of you need to participate.

Once you know you love each other, it's tempting to dismiss the other four questions. That's why you need to snap out of it, lover boy. Each question is weighted equally in the marriage test. So lose the googly-eyes and pay attention. Otherwise you may find yourself in divorce court. And that's where you'll get screwed more than you did on your honeymoon.

Chapter 50

If All Else Fails:
How to Live Happily Ever After

Storybook endings are romantic, impractical fictions that have nothing to do with real life. Real life is full of hardships and unpredictable changes. But although there is no magic formula for happiness, there are ways to minimize unhappiness. You don't want to be that old couple who seethe with hate and say nothing to each other.

The three things you should do to keep your marriage happy are compromise, put up with her little foibles, and maintain a healthy sex life.

1 Compromise
Marriage is a series of trade-offs. You listen to her ramble about the inept girl in her office, and she'll let you ramble on about how the Lions have no secondary. You go with her to the opera, and she'll go with you to the wrestling expo. Showing her that you're willing to do things for her shows you care about her. The key is making sure that what you give up does not exceed what you get. That way, when she's especially frustrating or annoying, you can take solace in the knowledge that the balance is at least tipping in your favor.

2 Put Up with It
Okay, so the things you thought were cute idiosyncrasies when you were dating are now clearly glaring character flaws: Her sleep time sniffles have become annoying snorts that keep you up. Her lips move when she reads. She always hums the same damn song when she does the dishes. She vacuums the rug in short steps rather than using the more efficient long sweep. If you can't get her to change whatever

it is that infuriates you, you have to put up with it. You've made your choice, now live with it. If you concentrate on the positive aspects, the negative aspects won't be so glaring. Presumably, there was a reason you walked down the aisle with this person, so try and focus on that. Visual aids can be helpful. If you married her for her looks, stare at her silently as your eyes work over her up and down, up and down. Ah, that's better. If you married her for money, visualize that fish-

ing boat in the garage or a giant pile of money. If you married her because her father was holding a shotgun, then concentrate on the image of you not being dead.

And find comfort in that age-old bumper-sticker adage: Someone, some-place, has it way worse than you.

Visualization can be helpful when employing the Put Up with It method.

③ Good Sex

Here are a few suggestions on how to keep a healthy sex life after several years of same old, same old:

- Have sex in a semipublic place. (Disregard if over sixty-five.)

- Role-play. She's the sexy nurse and you're the war hero who is paralyzed everywhere but . . . down there. (This has the added benefit of getting you out of any reciprocation.)

- Watch an adult movie, close eyes, go into bedroom.

- Forced one-month abstinence (including self-pleasure). Afterward, you'll be so ready that you'd hump a pile of sand if it got too close.

- Think about that girl you saw jogging in the park. Let's call her Cindi with an i.

- Uncomfortable strip tease followed by laughter and, aw, screw it, let's order Chinese.

It doesn't have to be fancy. Make it your own and mix it up every once in a while. Sex should be fun, and when it starts being a chore, you know you're doing something wrong. (Or it means you're in the porn business. If so, keep up the good work.)

Section XIV
The End of the Affair

Humanity has done many things. We've built the Great Wall of China, the Pyramids of Giza, and the skyscrapers of our modern cities. We've climbed the highest peaks, plumbed the depths of the oceans, mastered subatomic particles, and left footprints on the moon. The only challenge we haven't conquered is figuring out how to patch up a relationship when two people don't want to be together anymore.

Sometimes you have to accept the truth: The bloom is off the rose. There is no way you can reconcile. You've made your decision: She's gotta go.

Chapter 51

The Four Methods of Breaking Up

Breaking up is not hard to do. The Overachieving Underperformer employs four basic methods.

❶ The Band-Aid Technique

Sometimes you have to end a relationship quickly. It's painful but it's fast, like ripping off a Band-Aid. This method is for those of you who don't want

the relationship to linger just because you're too chicken to pull the trigger.

You don't want to hide behind phone calls, e-mails, or text messages. It's always best to break up face-to-face, so be a man and step up. Plus, face-to-face has an air of finality and gives the relationship closure.

All you have to say is, "I'm sorry, this isn't working out for me. This relationship is over." Inevitably she's going to ask why. Be honest. "I hate every fiber of your being." Or, "Every time I look at you, I want to kill myself." Remember, you don't

"Hi. We're through."

want to leave any unanswered questions. You want it over and you want her gone.

Tie up any loose ends. Make sure you put together a bag of her things so she never has a reason to drop by. Don't answer the phone when she calls, and stay away from her neighborhood, her workplace, or the bars she frequents for at least two months. You don't want to run into her, or any of her friends who may want to skin you alive.

❷ The Slow, Torturous Drift Apart

The slow, torturous drift apart is only recommended for guys dating a woman of questionable mind—a Psycho Chick (see Chapter 13). Drag the relationship on for months, gradually growing apart so as not to upset the careful balance that is her brain chemistry.

Slowly become the opposite of what she likes. If she loves going to rock shows, get into classical music. If she loves watching old movies, tell her you prefer everything colorized. Adopt political stances that you know she opposes. Hate everything she loves. Become the anti-her.

She will eventually approach you: "You're becoming a different person. You're not the guy I met three months ago." And that's when you

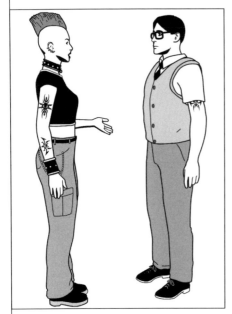

"You've...changed."

compare and contrast how different you both truly are. Suggest a trial separation, and you're home free.

③ The Other Woman

One definite way to end a relationship is to be caught with another woman. Don't literally be caught with your pants down, just making sure she knows there's someone else is sufficient. After that, she'll want to kill you, and then she'll want to dump you.

There doesn't even have to be a real other woman. Evidence of your cheating could be as simple as a matchbook with a phone number scrawled in it and left carelessly on the coffee table for her to find. A late night phone call. The smell of perfume. These can all be faked. Disappearing for hours with no explanation works too.

When she confronts you, let her know that you met someone and that although you haven't taken it anywhere romantically, you can't deny that you've thought about it. She'll take it from there, trust me. Just make sure everything around you is nailed down so she can't throw it at you.

The ten dollars for a prop bra that you stuff between the sofa cushions could be the best money you'll ever spend. Bigger cup size equals bigger outrage.

④ Get Her to Do It

The get-her-to-do-it method is for the man who is extremely afraid of conflict. If you want to avoid doing the dirty work of ending a relationship yourself, you have to trick your girlfriend into breaking up with you.

The execution of the get-her-to-do-it is simple; all you need to do is be as mean as you can. Don't worry, it will come naturally. Tell her you don't like the way she looks, dresses, or carries that extra ten pounds. Never be there when she needs you. Return her phone calls sporadically or never. Basically, be a jerk. If she has an ounce of self-respect, she will tire of your cadlike behavior and dump you. If not, then this is not the appropriate method, and you're likely better off using the Band-Aid technique.

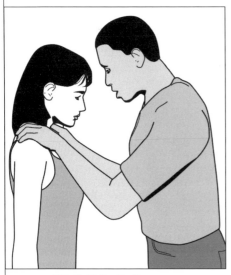

"Well, if that's the way it has to be . . ."

You know you've succeeded when your girlfriend tells you, "We need to talk." Sit there and take it when she proceeds to list your faults and the many reasons why she is pulling the plug and vowing never to be involved with you again. Try not to smile.

Remember, no matter what method you use to end the relationship, you want her a little mad at you so she'll keep away. But not so mad that she slashes your tires or ignites your golf bag.

Chapter 52

The Biggest Mistake:
Post-Breakup Sex and How to Do It

First, an advisory: Never, never, never, never, never, never, never have sex with an ex girlfriend after you've made your breakup official. There was a reason the relationship ended. Roll that thought around in your mind as you ponder one last mattress dance.

Why? It's obvious. She could take it as a sign that you're back together, and then you'll just have to hurt her again.

All that being said, you wouldn't be a man if the thought of one last taste after you've ended it didn't occur to you. But if you've dumped her correctly, she should want nothing to do with you. How do you slay this dragon?

- Be in the right place at the right time. Wear the shirt she bought you and "coincidentally" show up at the bar she always goes to. Alcohol reduces inhibitions, and it also helps her forget that you dumped her on New Year's Eve.

- Become more attractive. Lose ten pounds, cut your hair the way she always wanted you to, lift weights, dress better—anything that makes you seem better looking than you were when you were together.

- Be seen with another woman. Women are territorial, even after they throw their old territory's belongings in the yard and tell him to stay the hell away. If she sees you with a pretty woman (it doesn't have to be a date), she will become jealous. You just became more desirable.

- Make your case. Ask to speak to her for a minute, pull her aside, and tell her how much you miss her. Recall a specific moment in your past that was great. A powerful positive memory should trigger warm feelings in her.

- Close the deal. Be careful not to verbalize that you're going to be going home together. Articulating your intentions makes them more explicit and introduces openings for hesitation. Don't say, do.

When the tryst is over, make sure you let her know that this was a one-time thing and perhaps a mistake. You should be wearing your shoes when you say this so you can make a quick exit.

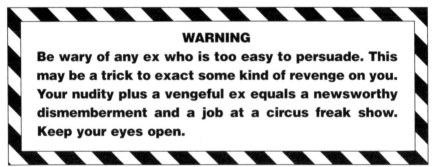

WARNING
Be wary of any ex who is too easy to persuade. This may be a trick to exact some kind of revenge on you. Your nudity plus a vengeful ex equals a newsworthy dismemberment and a job at a circus freak show. Keep your eyes open.